Master Pieces

THE ARCHITECTURE OF CHESS

Master Pieces

THE ARCHITECTURE OF CHESS

Gareth Williams

VIKING
STUDIO

For Vel

VIKING STUDIO

Published by the Penguin Group
Penguin Putnam Inc., 375 Hudson Street,
New York, New York 10014 U.S.A.

Penguin Books Ltd., 27 Wrights Lane,
London W8 5TZ, England

Penguin Books Australia Ltd., Ringwood,
Victoria, Australia

Penguin Books Canada Ltd.,
10 Alcorn Avenue,
Toronto, Ontario, Canada M4V 3B2

Penguin Books (N.Z.) Ltd.,
182-90 Wairan Road,
Aukland 10, New Zealand

Penguin Books Ltd., Registered Offices:
Harmondsworth, Middlesex, England

First Published in the United States
by Viking Studio,
a member of Penguin Putnam Inc.

First Printing, November 2000

10 9 8 7 6 5 4 3 2 1

A QUINTET BOOK

This book was designed and produced by
Quintet Publishing Limited
6 Blundell Street
London N7 9BH

Senior Project Editor: Laura Price
Editor: Andrew Armitage
Designers: Ian Hunt, Sharanjit Dhol
Photographer: John Melville
Illustrator: Richard Burgess

Creative Director: Richard Dewing
Publisher: Oliver Salzmann

Typeset in Great Britain by
Central Southern Typesetters, Eastbourne
Manufactured in Hong Kong by Regent Pte Ltd.
Printed in China by Midas Printing Ltd.

ISBN: 0-670-89381-1

CONTENTS

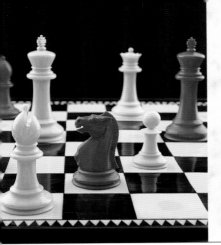

O thou, whose cynic sneers express
The censure of our favorite chess,
Know that its skill is science' self,
Its play distraction from distress,
It soothes the anxious lover's care,
It counsels warriors in their art,
When dangers threat and perils press:
And yealds us, when we need them most,
Companions in our loneliness.
—*Ibn Al-Mutazz, circa 1040*

INTRODUCTION

Chess is normally regarded as a game of bloodless battles, a conflict of intellectual thought, between two adversaries, each controlling a miniature army on a battlefield of 64 squares. Yet this is not the only aspect of chess that has enthralled participants over the centuries. The development and form of the chessmen, with their captivating seductiveness, have stimulated the imaginations of artists, craftsmen and designers in every country, on every continent, and in all cultures where the game of chess has been played. From virtually every society the design and style of these warriors of modest stature has reflected the spirit and culture of their environment.

Since the earliest recorded period, circa A.D. 600, these miniature soldiers have been made in a "figural" form for use as conventional chess sets or wholly as decorative artifacts that can on occasion be used, with care, to play a game. The great majority of conventional

BELOW *Early English Valentine card, circa 1910. Indicating the romantic chess connection. Since the Middle Ages chess was the only game allowed to be played between lovers without a chaperone.*

My little Love, do you remember,
Ere we grew so sadly wise,
When you and I played
chess together
Checkmated by each
other's eyes?

To my Valentine

chess sets made in quantity for play are of an "abstract" design, but these also have an artistic quality. An example of a decorative figural set would be a set representing the American War of Independence, a theme that remains popular on both sides of the Atlantic. One side portrays soldiers in the blue uniforms of the Continental Army, led by their commander-in-chief George Washington, opposed by the celebrated Red Coats of Britain's King George III's army.

Much more abundant are the conventional sets, economically designed chessmen in abstract style for practical use. A popular example is the Staunton set (named after Howard Staunton, of whom we'll see more later). This set was selected in 1924 by the World Chess Federation to be used in all international tournaments. However, the variety for abstract design in chess sets is infinite. Each country has manufactured conventional sets providing a selection of varying designs. Generally, the sets are well made, mainly carved or turned

THE CHALLENGE — Which hand, right or left?

THE STRUGGLE, — Intense Anxiety.

from wood or bone. This is clearly demonstrated within this book, with examples from the ancient Asian cultures to the relatively modern chess-set designs being used for serious competitive chess in today's world. Most of the chess sets illustrated date from the middle of the eighteenth century. Some were produced in established ivory carving areas of the time, like Berhampur in northeast India, Canton in China, Dieppe in France or Kholmogory in Russia. The schools of carving in these countries had their own traditional patterns, themes and distinctive carving styles which were often produced over many generations. Many European cities and towns also developed distinct designs for their chess sets, such as ones that are recognized as having been made in Lyons, Munich, Nuremberg and London. These sets were usually turned from wood, bone, or ivory, manufactured in quantity by skilled craftsmen whose pride in their work insured that quality was also an ingredient of their chessmen. These sets would mainly be sold locally in their own vicinity, although some of the larger well established work shops did export their sets to neighboring countries.

ABOVE *Entitled "The Struggle", this is a typical early nineteenth-century strip cartoon conveying the changing expressions of the players as the*

THE VICTORY.— Check-Mate!

THE PARTING.— Triumph & Chagrin.

game progresses, from jovial gamesmanship to concentration, to anger, and finally the inevitable conclusion —pleasure for the victor and melancholy for the loser.

LEFT *Chimpanzee against an Orangutan. A charming 1924 sketch by animal artist A.J. Shepherd displaying two intelligent members from the monkey family with an unsolvable problem —whose move it is!*

Individual artists, carvers and sculptors often chose to commemorate great historical events through their craft. Many fine figural chess sets were sculpted by master craftsmen and talented artists. Unfortunately, there is no tradition for such aesthetic creations to be signed, or recorded, in any organized manner. Many chess sets have been made by carvers to the highest artistic level and although greatly admired, the skilled artiste originators of these chess sets have to remain unknown and are not given the personal credit and respect their masterpieces so well deserve. Since the first half of the last century, when abstract

RIGHT *Woody Allen, a keen chess player, is seen here having an animated conversation over a chess game in the film,* The Front.

art became accepted by society, chess sets in this genre have become a common motif for modern artists. The Dadaist Man Ray (1890–1976) was among the first to create chess sets based on abstract design, with the dual intention of producing an artistic article with a practical purpose. His initial enterprise has inspired following generations of artists to create some outstanding and imaginative artworks, including many examples of chess sets.

The chronological presentation of the chess sets emphasizes the role of chess in art and design and shows the cultural influences that have played a major factor in the sets' final form. It also provides an unfamiliar insight into the progress of society since the earliest civilizations to the present time, touching on forgotten historical events and providing cameo insights to the famous and infamous characters from the past. The future is touched by the graphics of the computer, converting the three-dimensional pieces of the past into the two-dimensional graphics of a computer future, with a promise of possible infinite "choices" or "moves."

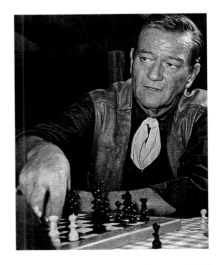

Since the eighteenth century chess sets have been created by the foremost ceramic companies. Meissen have produced attractive sets since the latter part of the eighteenth century, designed by Germany's leading artists, some of these early sets, such as the Saracen design are still being manufactured. Wedgwood soon followed with their jasperwear set created by Flaxman, based on Shakespearean plays. Since those early experimental days, the ceramic industry has expanded and developed. Ceramic products are now available in a great variety of goods among which are figural chess sets. Most ceramic sets are well designed and provide an interesting and varied choice of pleasant chess sets.

LEFT *English actors Peter Finch and Sir John Gielgud play a game of chess with an ivory carved Chinese chess set in the 1972 film* Lost Horizon. *Also starring in the film were Liv Ullman, Michael York, and Charles Boyer.*

Chapter I

THE ISLAMIC IMPACT

"If a ruler does not understand chess, how can he rule over a kingdom?"
—*Sassanian King of Kings, Khusros II, circa A.D. 600*

The Sanskrit name for chess is *Chaturanga*, which means the four divisions of an Indian army: chariots (represented by the rook/castle in the familiar chess set of today), cavalry (knight), elephants (bishop), and foot soldiers (pawns); added to these were a shah (king). When Alexander the Great invaded India around 327 B.C., he was astonished at the first sight of the Indian army that opposed him. Raja Porus had 50,000 foot soldiers, 1,000 chariots, 130 war elephants and 3,000 horsemen under his command. Alexander was looking at living chess set.

There is only speculative evidence, however, as to when chess started. A Persian manuscript, *Shahnama* ("Book of Kings"), recalls a legend of the sixth century of how a raja of India sent an envoy laden with precious gifts as a tribute to a powerful Persian king, Shah Khusrau Nushirwan, with a message presented on silk. One of the gifts was a magnificent game board, complete with pieces. The message contained a challenge to the wise men at the Persian court: they had to discover how this Indian game was played. If they succeeded, the raja would substantially increase his

BELOW *Afrasiab chessmen, carved ivory pieces from the seventh to eighth centuries: left to right—two soldier pawns carrying shields and short swords. Two mounted knights with shields and swords. A war elephant (bishop) wearing chain armour, carrying a warrior in full battle dress. A vizier seated on two horses with armed rider, and the Shah sitting on a three-horse chariot holding the emblem of power, a mace.*

LEFT AND PREVIOUS
PAGE *The Isle of
Lewis Chessmen,
discovered in 1931.
Chessmen from the
twelfth century,
carved from walrus
ivory. The group
consists of, from the
left top: a bishop
wearing his miter,
carrying his crozier
and wearing a cloak;
a bearded, crowned
king, seated on a
throne holding a
sword of authority
across his knees; a
crowned queen with
her right hand
touching her cheek; a
Norman knight
mounted on his steed
holding a shield.
Lower pieces from the
right: a warrior
armed with shield
and sword, and two
boundary stones
representing pawns.*

tribute to the shah; on the other hand, if the wise men failed to solve the puzzle, then the payment would be reversed and a substantial tribute would be demanded by the raja.

The challenge was accepted. The Shah's wisest vizier, Bozorgmehr, studied the problem for a day and a night before he announced his solution: "The board is a battlefield, the shah takes a position, with his army on either flank, and his vizier by his side, the soldiers line up in front, positioned ready to advance. The elephants are posted to the shah's side. Next to them are the war horses and on either side of these are the chariots. A complete army display in combat formation."

Bozorgmehr also indicated the move that each piece could make. He had won the challenge and the Indian raja had to pay the promised tribute to the shah.

The Afrasiab Chessmen

In 1977 an expedition from the Uzbekistan Academy of Archaeology conducting a controlled dig in Afrasiab, Samarqand, discovered seven miniature ivory carvings of chess pieces: a shah, a vizier, a chariot, an elephant, two armed horsemen and a foot soldier. These figures are particularly small averaging only $1^1/_4$ inches in height. They date from the seventh century and are the earliest figural chess pieces to be authenticated.

Samarqand in the seventh century was an advanced civilization, with a stable society and a developed aesthetic culture. The discovery in Afrasiab of these chessmen has added extra

archaeological evidence to the sparse historical documentation that exists from this period. From the style of workmanship displayed and the skill of carving shown in these miniature figures, it can be surmised that they were carved in a conventional style from an established tradition—a tradition that must have been in existence for decades, and more likely centuries before the pieces were made. The chessmen also provide new and important information on the structure and formation of a Central Asian army. A *pieda* (pawn) is shown as a soldier, on one knee, holding a shield and sword, ready for action. The chariot (rook) is pulled by three horses, two with riders, one as the charioteer and the other as a warrior, armed with sword and shield.

The shah (king) is seated high on a throne, placed on a grand carriage, being drawn by three horses. The *asp* (horse/knight) has an armed warrior mounted, while the *pil* (elephant/bishop), is covered in chain armor and is ridden by a mahout, also in armor. The *ferz* (queen), the shah's adviser, is shown mounted and armed.

The Influence of Islam

These carved ivory chessmen have provided an authentic representation of an Asian army, similar to the one faced by Alexander a thousand years earlier, and they illustrate clearly the figural form of chess pieces used for playing, thought to be the original form of chess.

When Muslim armies occupied Iran in the seventh century, they adopted many of the customs and institutions of the more cultivated nation they had conquered. Among these was *shatranj* (the Arabic name for chess). The game spread rapidly through the expanding Islamic Empire. By A.D. 950 it was well established in the Arab world. Caliphs kept resident chess players at their courts. The best known of these was as-Suli. Known as a player of remarkable skill, he was the chess master at the court of Baghdad in the reign of Caliph al-Muktafi (902–908). The chess pieces he played with were of an abstract design. Such chessmen were discovered by an Iranian archaeological expedition undertaken by

ABOVE *Iranian ninth-century ivory rook from Nishapur. This early abstract shape is a stylized silhouette of a contemporary war chariot.*

New York's Metropolitan Museum of Art in 1939 to Nishapur in northeast Iran. They date from the ninth century and are probably the first example of abstract minimalist art.

The elephants of the Raja and Vizier are reduced to a carved block of ivory representing three differing aspects of the piece. The lower section indicates the bulk of the elephant; the higher recessed section is the throne; and the small protrusion represents the head of the raja or vizier. The elephants (bishops) are a simple block of ivory with two small protrusions from the upper part to indicate tusks. The simplified silhouette of a horse is easy to recognize and the cleft shape of the rook would have been easily identified by players in the ninth century as the outline of a war chariot.

The pawn, dome-shaped, is the smallest piece, attesting to its military rank.

ABOVE *Lebanese glass games piece, tenth century, possibly a chess king or queen.*

FAR RIGHT *Fourteenth-century king or queen made from Yorkshire jet, excavated on the site of central England's 1970s new town, Milton Keynes.*

RIGHT *Spain's King Alfonso the Wise, 1283 treatise, "Game of Chess, Dice and Boards," contains instructions about many indoor games. This is one of the illustrations from Alfonso's work describing chess.*

LEFT *Chessmen excavated from the river Thames, fourteenth century, bone and wood. From the top left to right: bone king, wood king, unidentified chess man due to poor condition, bishop, side view, showing protrusions symbolising the tusks of an Indian elephant. Second row, left to right: front view of bishop piece, bone king, side view and then viewed from above, showing the hollow bone structure.*

Chess in its Islamic form had reached Spain by the tenth century, having been introduced there by the Moors. By the twelfth century chess was firmly established as a favorite pastime in the feudal culture of Europe. The game preserved its Persian rules and the abstract design of chessmen maintained their Arabian nomenclature: *shah*/king, *firzan* /queen, *fil* /bishop, *faras*/knight, *rukh*/rook/castle, and *baidaq* /pawn.

Numerous chess pieces of similar abstract form to the Nishapur chessmen, and dated from the tenth to fourteenth centuries, have been found in major centers throughout Europe. The Count of Urgel willed Crystal chessmen to the church in Ager, Spain, in 1010. Ivory chessmen at the Nuremberg Museum were discovered at a castle used in 1096–99 as a meeting point during the First Crusade. In the 1970s wooden chessmen from the fourteenth century were excavated from the Thames river bed in London, England, by the Department of Urban Archaeology of the London Museum.

RIGHT *Seven twelfth-century Isle of Lewis, walrus ivory chessmen. Clockwise from the left: a bishop, a king, a queen, a knight, a pawn, another pawn, and a warrior rook.*

Although the Koran does not specifically condemn the practice of carving figures, it has always been discouraged within its culture. Thus, chesspieces were less likely to be figurative and the carving instead favored geometrical design. Therefore the prevailing shape of the early chessmen conveniently conformed with the concepts of the Islamic religion.

The Lewis Chessmen

In Christian Europe, the situation was different: carving was an essential craft required and encouraged in both the Gothic and Baroque architectural traditions. Magnificent works of art still adorn the cathedrals of the Middle Ages. Artisans of the early European carved sets had to adopt new names for the chessmen that would be acceptable and understood.

The Arabic shatranj names had no logical meaning in the nations of Christian Europe.

The Lewis chessmen at the British Museum provide a good example of such a set. Discovered on the Isle of Lewis, off the western coast of Scotland in 1831, they characterize a medieval Nordic army. Visually mysterious and attractive, they are also ideally balanced and proportioned as a set created to be used for play, as well as being decorative.

These Lewis chessmen, carved from walrus ivory, are an excellent example of good

ABOVE *William Golding, author of* Lord of the Flies *and winner of the 1983 Nobel prize for literature, considers the next move he should make on his Lewis chess set.*

LEFT *Lewis chessmen, from the left: knight, bishop, king, pawn, queen, and rook.*

BELOW LEFT *The Lewis rooks are foot soldiers, a number that glare as they bite their shields are "berserkers," Vikings that work themselves into a frenzy in order to fight courageously in battle. From the rear it can be seen that they wore chain armor that covered the whole body and they protected their front with a long shield adorned with primitive blazons, and a powerful sword.*

design, a chess set that is both aesthetic and practical—a twelfth-century army, personifying a royal court of the period: king, queen, bishop, and knight. A Viking "Berserker" warrior in place of a castle and boundary stones in place of pawns are the only difference between these ancient chessmen and a modern chess set. Recent investigation suggests that the Lewis chessmen may

have originated in Trondheim, the medieval capital city of Norway, and home to the Norsemen during the eleventh and twelfth centuries who were the overlords of the Isle of Lewis. It seems that they brought the chessmen with them from Norway when they voyaged to the island.

The pieces were discovered on the beach in the parish of Uig on the Isle of Lewis but mystery still surrounds the question of exactly where. A number of differing stories have emerged. One of the most plausible, and one of the quaintest, is that they were found by a local herdsman in a small brick oven on a sandbank. At first sight they must have appeared to him to be a group of gnomes or mythical "little people" stoically staring back at him. According to the story, the herdsman ran off in panic. Encouraged by his wife, he overcame his fear and superstition and returned to find that they were only little carved ivory figures.

BELOW *A king and pawn from the Charlemagne chessmen. The king, Emperor Alexis Comnen, is shown sitting on his throne, with an attendant on each side holding a curtain open. They are all within a secured small throne chamber, which provides protection from assassination attempts from the rear. The pawn is similar to the Lewis warrior rooks. He carries the long shield and wears the same style of helmet and chain armor. He is probably a Nordic soldier from Robert Quiscard's army.*

BELOW *In the
Eastern tradition the
war elephant
represents the bishop
in modern chess. Like
the soldiers, the
elephant is protected
with a full covering of
chain mail. There are
two riders: one is the
mahout, to control
the animal, leaving
the other rider free to
fight. The knight, on
the right, is another
Nordic soldier. Like
the Lewis knights he
carries a long shield
and a sword. There is
a Byzantium knight
among the
Charlemagne chess
pieces. He carries a
round shield and
wears a pudding
bowl helmet.*

The Charlemagne Chessmen

Another important historical group of medieval chessmen are at the Bibliothèque Nationale, Paris, France. Once believed to have been a gift to Emperor Charlemagne, they are now known to have been made in the eleventh century and originated in the Amalfi area of Southern Italy. Carved from African ivory, the major pieces are impressive in size and bulk (5–6 inches), consisting of two kings, two queens, three elephants, four knights, three chariots, and one pawn.

Yuri Averbakh, chess grandmaster and historian, when investigating the historical background of the Charlemagne chessmen, made the discovery that they recorded a real conflict between a Byzantium emperor and an ambitious Norman warlord—in particular Emperor Alexis Comnen and his

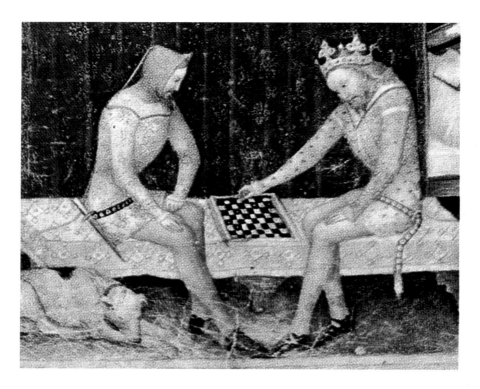

dominating ambitious mother, Queen Anna Dalassina. They fought against a conquering army of Nordic mercenaries led by Robert Quiscard, who was determined to reinstate the deposed Byzantium emperor, Michael Duca, who was married to Quiscard's daughter, Helena. The carved ivory kings seen seated on their thrones in the chess set, are the Emperors Alexis Comnen and Michael Duca, while the ivory queens represent Anna Dalassina and Helena.

It is significant that in the two earliest European chess sets carved in a representational form—the Lewis chessmen and the Charlemagne—introduce a queen as the natural companion to the king, replacing the Arabic vizier. The inclusion of elephants and chariots among the Charlemagne pieces suggests that chess may have been introduced to Eastern Europe through the Byzantium Empire.

ABOVE *A miniature drawing from a manuscript by Guiron le Courtois of Milan. Circa 1370-1380. This shows King Arthur of England enjoying a game of chess, possibly with one of the knights from his famous Round Table.*

"It is no time to be playing chess when the house is on fire."
—*Italian Proverb, circa 1550.*

The Renaissance, which started in Florence, Italy, in the fourteenth century and culminated there in the sixteenth century, is regarded as marking the period of transition from the Middle Ages to modern times. It was certainly during this period that many changes occurred to chess.

At the end of the fifteenth century, chess players in Spain and Italy started experimenting with the rules of the game, which had not altered significantly since chess arrived in Europe during the tenth century. The alterations to the rules included allowing the pawn to move two squares on its first move. The bishop's move was extended so that it could travel along the whole length of its diagonal. The queen, which at the time could move only one square diagonally, was given the freedom of the board, allowed, as now, to move in any direction as far as the board's perimeter.

The Spanish and French referred to this new game as "the queen's chess." The Italians were less courteous and called it "the mad queen's game." With these alterations the game became more tactical and exciting and it rapidly spread through Europe.

The nomenclature of the chessmen also changed. Most of the Arabic names were discontinued in favor of names in the language of the various European countries. The king and queen are constant, but there was variance with the bishop. In France it was known as a *fou*, jester to the king, in Germany as a messenger, and in Italy as a standard bearer or officer. In a number of countries the knight is referred to as a horse, while the rook/chariot has been transformed into a castle or tower. The pawn remains unchanged as a soldier.

The shape of the conventional playing sets also changed. The squat carved design of Nishapur, which had been so successful for over 500 years, gave way to the improved technology of the lathe.

ABOVE *English, early eighteenth-century ivory chess set made by turners on a lathe and finished by carving. The king is decorated with three crowns, possibly meant to represent the three crowns worn by the Pope, pointing to support of the subversive Jacobean cause for Catholics against the English Anglican monarchy of George I and George II.*

THE LANGUAGE OF CHESS

	ENGLISH	ARABIC	INDIAN	FRENCH	ITALIAN	SPANISH	GERMAN	DUTCH	RUSSIAN
king	king	shah	shah	roi	re	rey	konig	koning	korol
queen	queen	firzan	wazir	reine	regina	reina	konigin	koningen	ferz
bishop	bishop	fil	fil	fou	alfiere	alfil	laufer	raadsheer	slon
knight	knight	faras	asp	cavalier	cavaliere	caballo	springer	ridder	kon
rook	rook	rkhkh	rukh	tour	torre	torre	turm	kasteel	ladia
pawn	pawn	baidaq	piyada	pion	pedina	peon	bauer	pion	peshka

New Names for New Designs

One of the earliest examples of these new chess sets can be seen at the Ashmolean Museum, Oxford, England. This magnificent board with the original chessmen dates from around 1450. It was made in Florence by Baldassarre Embriachi, prince of carvers and carver to princes. Embriachi invented a way of preparing and carving bone so that it could be used like ivory. The Ashmolean board is a good representative example of the quality of his work.

SHATRANJ 600AD
SHATRANJ 7TH CENTURY
SHATRANJ 8TH CENTURY
SHATRANJ 9TH CENTURY
SHATRANJ LATER

LEFT *A map showing the movement and development of the old game of chess (shatranj) up to 1200 A.D. The game was known in the northwest of India in the sixth century when it was introduced to Persia. After the Arabic conquest of Persia the game spread throughout the Islamic Empire. By the eighth century chess was popular with the caliphs of Baghdad and had reached Medina and Mecca. From there, the Arabs took the game through Syria, into North Africa, and along the North African coast. It was introduced into Spain by the Moors, and it quickly spread throughout Western Europe, reaching England in the eleventh century. In the East, shatranj passed from India into Mongolia at the beginning of the seventh century, and from there to Russia. The game also spread from India to Sumatra and on to Borneo, Java, and Malaya. It seems likely that the Chinese game is a modified version of the Indian game and that Japan received the game from Korea in the thirteenth century.*

Chessmen from this period are very rare, as only a few have survived. The Embriachi chessmen were turned on a lathe from bone and horn, and provide a rare and early example of the upright design produced by this method.

For the next 500 years almost all chess sets of a conventional design would have been made by turners working on their lathes. The basic outline of the set is simple and clear. The king and queen continue the Islamic tradition of being similar, distinguished only by height difference, the king being the taller.

ABOVE *Some of the main chess pieces from the Embriachi board, starting from the left—turned from bone—a pawn, bishop, queen, and rook. Turned from horn—rook, queen, bishop, and pawn. There is a king with the set, the same design as the queens but taller.*

LEFT *A top view of the Embriachi chessboard, showing the elaborately decorative carving of the bone surround and the hidden drawer containing the chess pieces.*

The bishop/standard bearer is shown as a shield. Unfortunately, no knights have remained: they may have been a stylized horse heads or abstractly "cut aslope" as though having been knighted. The pawns are simple thimble shapes, but the rook is exotic, bird-shaped. Some countries believed the rook to be a mythical monster bird, and possibly this is its representation here—or maybe this shape for a rook created the mythical bird!

Very few chessmen still exist from this period. However, it is possible to obtain a visual impression of the form for conventional chessmen from contemporary literature and paintings. Woodcuts from Dr. V. Mennol's 1520 book confirm clearly that European chess is now based on the cultural structure of a medieval society ruled by a monarchy. The drawings illustrate the chessmen in a form that would be acceptable for a master carver to create, while also providing two abstract designs for each piece that can be used by a turner for making a conventional playing chess set. The translations of the names are written underneath the drawings in medieval German. The king, queen, and knight are established; there is uncertainty about the others, being shown here as a scholar (bishop), judge (rook), and peasant (pawn).

The Game of Kings

Sculptors and carvers of the Renaissance period had reached an unsurpassable standard of technical excellence in the skills of craftsmanship. This remarkable quality in the presentation of the set and the skill of carving displayed by each individual chess piece is of such a high standard that such a set could possibly have been commissioned by a member of the Florentine Medici family.

Around the year 1510, Vida, Bishop of Alba, wrote a poem entitled "The Game of Chess." In it he introduced some changes in the nomenclature for some of the pieces. He used the word *archers* (bishop) in place of the Arabic *fil* (elephant). And for *rukh*, he introduced "Elephant and Castle." In this set Vida's elephant, with castle, is impressively represented by a talented Renaissance artist. His bishops and pawns are in the style of Donatello's *David*, a bronze, circa 1430, made for Cosimo de Medici (1389–1464). The headwear of the kings and queens portrays the fashion of period. The knight is carved as a rearing horse and all the pieces are presented on decorative ormolu mounts.

New chess soon had its chess masters. In 1575 a match was played at the court of King Philip II of Spain in Madrid. The contesting chess masters were Spain's Ruy Lopez de Segura, a

BELOW *A superb example of Renaissance artistry. Carved from ivory this set displays the essence of quality for the period. The rook, exquisitely carved and presented as a castle tower carried by an elephant, became the traditional symbol for figural sets throughout Europe during the following centuries. The pawn is carved in the style of Donatello's bronze of David, at the Museo Nazionale Del Bargello, Florence.*

priest, who had in 1561 published *Libro de la invencion liberal y arte juego del Axedrez*. Ruy Lopez was the Spanish court's regular chess master, and considered at the time to be the best player of the Spanish Empire. His talented opponent was Italy's Giovanni Leonardo di Bono from Cutro in Calabria, commonly known as "Il Puttino," an affectionate term referring to his small stature. The rules for the match were simple: the first to win three games would be the winner.

The prestige of being acclaimed the finest chess player in the Spanish Empire would be enormous. The prize was a most generous reward given by Philip II, the richest and most powerful monarch in Christendom. Leonardo lost his first two games and had to plead, on his knees, for the King to stay for the remainder of the match, saying, "I beg Your Majesty not to go, for that which I have done has been purposely contrived to display my skill the more clearly. Your Majesty will behold that, of the following games, I shall win them all and that without much difficulty. This I undertake to perform on pain of losing my life."

Leonardo did win the following games and became the "supreme Chess Champion."

In the sixteenth century there are records from England's Henry VIII's inventory showing he owned "boxes and bags of chessmen, graven [carved] in bone or of black and white bone." Henry (1491–1547) had a collection of at least 11 chess sets. Most were carved out of bone and kept in satin bags or black leather boxes. Unfortunately, none of these have survived.

A design similar to that of the chess sets current during Henry's reign can be seen in an oil painting of 1568. It shows Lord Windsor and his family with two of his sons playing chess. The

pieces can be seen quite clearly: they are probably bone, having been turned on a lathe—even the knight, which is shown "cut aslope" as described in James Rowbothum's 1562 book on chess. There is no rook shown on the board to indicate if the tower or castle has yet replaced the mythical bird.

During the 1700's the style of chessmen shown in the Windsor family painting were to continue, but gradually some significant

BELOW *English conventional playing set, illustrating the six main pieces that constitute a chess set: king, queen, bishop, knight, rook and pawn. Turned and carved in ivory, one side stained black. It might be a Jacobean set, a most unusual feature, being the king with three crowns carved on to its stem, possibly signifying allegiance to the Pope.*

evolving and improving the designs of European chess sets. The rook became established as a tower or castle. This may have been influenced by Vida's chess poem, *Scacchia Ludus*, which describes the rook as an elephant with a tower. Certainly in figural sets the elephant and castle has become a traditional symbol for the rook; the castle, easily turned, has come off Vida's elephant's back and stands alone in the conventional playing set. The set shown on page 48 (top) illustrates the development of these changes.

The set is turned from ebony and ivory. The king, queen, and pawns are similar in shape to the Windsor chess pieces. However, the bishop has a cut across its rounded finial to suggest a miter; the knight differs in that here it has a carved triangle-shaped finial, possibly to represent a squire's tricorn hat; the castle has arrived— it is well turned and has been finished with surface cutting to portray the stonework, and a domed roof completes it. This set has no provenance, but, from the technique of turning and its pattern, a reasonable deduction should place it in the late 1600s.

Another set, shown below, dating from around 1710, introduces the knight as a stylized horse's head, and a bishop with a conspicuous miter. Both these, the bishop and the horse, have— particularly in Anglo-American chess sets—become established members of the chess army. There is also an unusual feature in the design of the king: three crowns have been added on to king's column. This may indicate that this was a Jacobite set. A three-tiered crown as represented on the king is the symbol of the Holy Roman Catholic Empire and was worn by the Pope.

At the time the Catholic Jacobites were at variance with the English throne. In 1715 a Jacobian revolt to overthrow King George I was defeated.

By the 1750s the basic foundation for the modern design of an English chess set was complete. For the first time a conventional playing set was designed with a king represented by a crown, a queen by a coronet, a bishop by a miter, a knight by a horse, and a rook by a castle tower. These sets were turned from bone, one side being stained black, and appear by design to have come from one particular turner's workshop. They also produced sets with one side stained red, which provides an indication of when the red and white fashion for coloring chess sets began.

It was to be another hundred years, however, before the variety in design of playing sets would begin to conform to one particular standard for chessmen.

ABOVE *A nineteenth-century painting of two eighteenth-century noblemen playing chess with a French ivory "Regency" set. The white king should be mated on the next move, but the position on the board is illegal, the king being in check by both the red queen and the red knight. An impossible position in chess!*

And lastly, we learn by chess the habit of not being discouraged by present bad appearances in the state of our affairs; the habit of hoping for a favorable chance, and that of persevering in the search of resources."

—*Benjamin Franklin, "The Morals of Chess" (article), 1786*

Benjamin Franklin (1706–90) was an eminent statesman, printer, author, and scientist. He also had a passion for chess. He wrote in his autobiography of how, in 1733, he found that playing chess distracted him from his foreign-language studies. To resolve this problem he agreed with his opponent that the winner would set a study task for the loser, which, upon his honor, would be completed before their next game.

The first chess article published in the U.S.A. was Franklin's "The Morals of Chess." It appeared in the *Columbian* magazine in 1786, and praised the game that was such a distraction to the distinguished man. It has been widely reprinted since, and was also published in the first American textbook on chess in 1802.

ABOVE AND PREVIOUS PAGE *German ivory and ebony set made by a master turner, proving that conventional designs for sets can also be considered as artistic abstract sculptures when created by experienced master craftsmen. The set is dated circa 1840, with the height of the king at 4 inches.*

RIGHT Benjamin Franklin playing chess with Lady Howe, London 1774.

BELOW A late eighteenth-century wood French "Regency" set similar in design to one owned by Benjamin Franklin. For convenience all the chessmen have been turned, the traditional horse's head for the knight being omitted, thereby saving the manufacturer the cost of employing a skilled carver. This is a typical French playing set of the eighteenth century. The abstract design is very neutral, an astute marketing ploy so as not to discourage their sales to various continuously volatile political and religious factions within.

As American envoy in England he was ostensibly invited to play a social game of chess with Lady Howe at her home. The game, however, provided an opportunity to meet her brother Lord Howe, a Member of Parliament, to discuss the difficult situation developing with Britain, in the hope that war could be prevented.

The year 1779 saw Franklin in Paris, where he made the acquaintance of another chess-playing woman companion, Madame Brillon. Their passion for chess was such that on one occasion they played while Madame Brillon was in her bath!

Two of Franklin's chess sets still exist from this period. One is a conventional wooden playing set, well worn with a genuine patina, which obviously served its owner well. The other is a very attractive ivory miniature set of the same design but impossible to play with; possibly from one of his female companions.

George Washington (1732–99), the first president of the United States and commander-in-chief of the victorious Continental Army against the British in the War of Independence, was another chess player among the founding fathers. An ivory chess set of his was kept at his home, Mount Vernon, and is now at the United States National Museum, Washington. The set is English and, partly because of the provenance of the president's set, can reasonably be dated to around 1770.

Whoever decided to introduce the color red to oppose white not only created an attractive color combination but also ensured patriotic patronage from a potential source of major customers, namely the English gentry.

The design of the set has evolved from the culture of the Middle Ages when the monarch and his queen were all-powerful, morally supported by the church—in this case Anglican bishops—and their knights, secured by their Norman castles, overseeing the enforcement of the king's laws with an army protecting the system against the enemy, from without or from within. Ironically, this was a political system that George Washington, with the support of his American colonists, was about to change.

There is a story that chess played a fortuitous cameo part in the destiny of Commander George Washington. The war against the British was not proceeding too well before the battle of Trenton, New Jersey. Washington decided to attack his enemies and surprise them by crossing the Delaware in appaling weather

BELOW *The Washington set—as this set is now known —was a relatively new design when Washington obtained it. Ivory and bone sets would normally have been black and white, the black side either dyed or made from ebony. Red and white are the colors of St. George, England's patron saint. Turned from ivory, with one side stained red, this was a popular style of set in England and among the gentry of the British Empire during the later part of the eighteenth century. The king and queen continue in the abstract tradition, the queen represented by a traditional sphere, the king, with an added geometrical finial suggesting a hat.*

conditions. A British sympathizer sent his son with a note the evening before the battle to warn the English army. Colonel Johann Rall was so engrossed in a game of chess that he carelessly pocketed the note. After the battle, the colonel was found mortally wounded, the note still in his pocket, unread. The Battle of Trenton is regarded by many historians as the turning point in the Revolutionary War.

Thomas Jefferson (1743–1826), third president of the United States and main author of the American Declaration of Independence, was, like Franklin, an enthusiastic chess player. In 1769 he wrote to Jack Walter suggesting that they relieve the pressure of diplomatic talks with a game of chess when they met at a forthcoming meeting in Williamsburg.

In his Jefferson's Memorandum Book there are a number of references to buying chess sets. In 1769 he gave one James Ogilvie 45 shillings to buy him a set of chessmen in Williamsburg. While in Philadelphia in 1783 he bought a set of chessmen for 37 shillings

ABOVE *George Washington leads his army across the treacherous Delaware river to take the British army by surprise at Trenton. A famous turning point in the American Revolutionary War.*

and paid a further 30 shillings for a chessboard. When visiting New York in 1784 he again records buying a set for only 11 shillings and 6 pence. Interested also in chess literature, he had in his library most of the published chess books available at the time.

Two incomplete chess sets from Jefferson's collection have survived. One is a French set, with carved ivory bust figures on turned baluster-shaped pedestals. One side, dyed red, represents Africans, the other a French royal court. The set was carved in Dieppe, which was renowned as a port of entry for African ivory and known as a thriving ivory center. The set was presented to Jefferson by the French government when he was in Paris as American Minister to France (1785–89). The kings are missing: could they have been deliberately omitted as not to embarrass

represent a European monarchy, opposed by African warriors. A similar set was presented to Thomas Jefferson by the French government when he was American minister to France. In Jefferson's set the kings have been removed, a symbolic gesture to the new Republican status of America and France.

the new minister from the recently formed republic? Or were they stolen by a Royalist sympathizer?

Jefferson's other remaining set is a conventional English "Barleycorn" bone set made by skilled turners working on lathes, finishing with surface carving in relief on the body of the royals. The colors, red and white, have by now become the traditional choice for English bone and ivory sets. The Barleycorn name derives from a turner's description for a symmetrical circular pattern as worked onto these chess sets. The Jefferson set with 5-inch kings is the finest of its kind. The visual impression created, particularly by the larger sets, is just majestic. This style of set proved to be very popular among the serious chess players of the nineteenth century, and the sets continued in production until World War I.

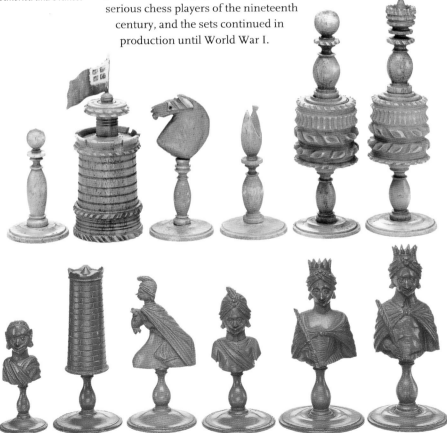

THE EXPANSION YEARS

"Pawns: they are the soul of this game, they alone form the attack and defense."
— *F.-A.D. Philidor, L'Analyze du Jeu des Échecs, 1748*

Chess in the eighteenth century was centered on France, particularly Paris, where a café society was emerging providing not only food and drinks but a relaxed ambiance, encouraging clientele to linger, meet their friends, read the papers, smoke a good cigar from the Indies, or enjoy a game, such as cards, checkers, backgammon, and chess. The most famous of these establishments was the Café de la Régence. Originally opened in 1670 by an American, it had by 1750 become a Mecca for chess players: Philidor, Bourdonnais, Saint-Amant, Staunton, Anderssen and, Paul Morphy, all great players who fought many a battle over the tables. Other celebrities who were regular clientele of the café included Voltaire, Rousseau, Robespierre, Franklin, Jefferson, and Napoleon.

Philidor, François-André Danican (1726–95), musician, composer, and master chess player, was loved by the English for his chess and by the French for his music. He first visited London in 1747 and impressed everyone

BELOW *French "Regency" set made from bone, one side stained brown. This was the most popular design of set from the mid-eighteenth century until the turn of the twentieth century. An inexpensive version was produced in wood and successfully exported in the nineteenth century to chess clubs and cafés throughout the French colonies, Europe and America. King 4 inches.*

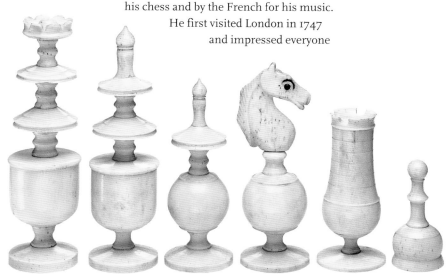

A caricature of Napoleon playing chess against Lord Cornwallis, 1802. It refers to treaty negotiations between Britain and France where Bonaparte completely out maneuvered Cornwallis. In the cartoon Napoleon states, "Check to your king, remember it is not the first time, and I think a few manoeuvres more will completely convince you that I am better acquainted with the game I am playing than you are aware of." Cornwallis replies, "Curse it, I shall lose this Game, you are too much for me." It was Cornwallis who in 1781 had to surrender his army of 7,000 men to the American colonies

Check to your King, remember it is not the first time, and I think a very few Manœuvres more will compleatly convince you that I am better acquainted with the Game I am playing than you are aware of.

Curse it I shall lose this Game; You are too much for me.

with his chess ability, comfortably beating the leading English players. He also visited Berlin and Potsdam, where he gave a display of blindfold chess in the presence of Prussia's King Frederick the Great, known to be a keen chess enthusiast.

Over many years Philidor successfully composed comic opera for the Parisian Opéra Comique.

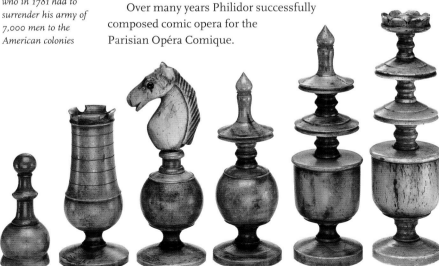

He also composed for the grand opera and ballet. His *Ernelinda, Princess of Norway* so delighted Louis XV that he awarded Philidor a pension from the king's privy purse of 25 Louis d'or.

In London in 1774, Parsloe's, an exclusive gentlemen's club, was formed. Membership was limited to 100, drawn from the gentry and nobles of high social rank. Among these were Charles Fox, Lord Mansfield, and General Burgoyne. Philidor was invited to be the club's resident chess master, and for 20 years, between the months of February and May, he would leave his family in Paris to attend Parsloe's in London.

Presumably because of Philidor's chess exploits, there was an upsurge of interest in the game. It seems to coincide with a general improvement in the quality of work produced by master craftsmen, including turners and carvers.

More ivory seems to be have become available and was used in the

LEFT *François-André Danican Philidor, regarded by many as the first modern chess master. His book* Analyse des Echecs *has been translated into many languages and produced in countless editions in its two hundred years. This portrait was used in 1777 as the frontispiece to the second edition.*

BELOW *French "Lyon" chessmen, nineteenth century. An attractive design due to the bone trimmings and finials, the king and queen with a stylized crown and coronet. Turned from wood, one side is stained reddish brown against black. King 4 inches.*

ABOVE *Eighteenth-century English chess men, from a set owned by Philidor and carried by him on his numerous journeys in Europe.*

ABOVE RIGHT The Chess Players, *a pastel drawing by Henry Edridge, 1810, of two English gentlemen, enjoying a game of chess played with an ivory and ebony set.*

making of high-quality artifacts, including chessmen. A number of new firms were established in London who made chess sets. Many designs of the late eighteenth century were developed and improved. John Calvert, a Master of the Worshipful Company of Turners, established his firm around 1795 and it continued until the mid 1800s. John Jaques also established his family firm at this time. John Jaques and Son, Ltd., are still trading, and in 1995 celebrated 200 years of continuous business.

Robert Carpenter of Bath was a Freeman of the City, artist and master carver. Bath is a city in the west of England, popular with tourists since the nineteenth century owing to the spa waters and ancient Roman baths.

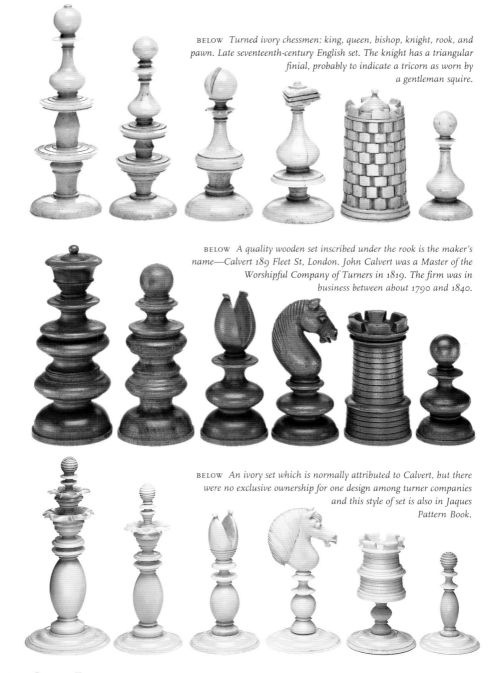

BELOW *Turned ivory chessmen: king, queen, bishop, knight, rook, and pawn. Late seventeenth-century English set. The knight has a triangular finial, probably to indicate a tricorn as worn by a gentleman squire.*

BELOW *A quality wooden set inscribed under the rook is the maker's name—Calvert 189 Fleet St, London. John Calvert was a Master of the Worshipful Company of Turners in 1819. The firm was in business between about 1790 and 1840.*

BELOW *An ivory set which is normally attributed to Calvert, but there were no exclusive ownership for one design among turner companies and this style of set is also in Jaques Pattern Book.*

The ebony side of the English set. The rook with the incisive cutting of the brickwork and the knight without the horse head are indications of an early set. King 3 inches.

This set has been turned from boxwood and rosewood to provide the opposing colors and dates from the early nineteenth century. The top of the king has now evolved into a shape that indicates a form of head wear.

By the nineteenth century coloring one side of an ivory set red had become the accepted tradition. The unusual form of the king and queen with their floral finials makes an attractive design. King 4 inches.

The city was also a trading port, importing from and exporting to North Africa. Saracens, dressed in their traditional clothing, wearing turbans, were a normal sight in the markets of Bath.

Robert Carpenter drew on these two contrasting cultures, Romans and Saracens, as the inspiration for the design of his chess sets (see page 56). It seems he may have worked with the artist Edward Bird, R.A., who had opened a drawing school in nearby Bristol and was a named painter to Princess Charlotte. Drawings Bird made for a chess set are of a similar design to Carpenter's sets. The drawings may have been used as the blueprint for the chess sets.

By the end of the eighteenth century, Robert Carpenter had developed his own distinctive style of carving. The main subjects of his ivory carvings were local domestic scenes, as his Saracen trader, seen displaying Oriental carpets to an affluent town lady. Carpenter's work was praised by George III's wife, Queen Charlotte, and her daughter, Princess Elizabeth. A local paper in 1817 reported that, "They [the Queen and Princess] inspected his unique pieces of sacred and historical sculpture and expressed

ABOVE *A painting by A. E. Chalon, R. A. Titled* The Approaching Check Mate *referring to the couple's pending marriage.*

BELOW *In the 1820s, fire damaged the thirteenth-century church of St. George, Windsor Castle. A turner in Eton used the old oak from the fire to make this souvenir set in a St. George design.*

ABOVE *Ceramic French faience set and board in a Regency style. Originally made in the late eighteenth century, the last few were made by Samson of Paris in the 1960s.*

RIGHT *Base view of the Oak Windsor set kings displaying labels with the inscription, "I. Parker—Eton—Turner to Her Majesty—Made from the old wood of Windsor Castle".*

most unqualified approbation of their execution." Other artistic work done by Carpenter were *The Decapitation of Lady Jane Gray* and *The Maid of Orleans*. After his death, believed to be around 1830, then over eighty years of age, he was mentioned in a biography as the "historical carver of great celebrity."

Surprisingly, a chess set by Carpenter was mistaken for the work of a French prisoner of the Napoleonic war. Prisoners were encouraged to earn money toward their keep by making artifacts out of bone, wood, and straw, which could

BELOW *Chess sets designed by Jaques in 1828 for using at Simpsons Chess Divan in the Strand, the Mecca for all the best chess players of*

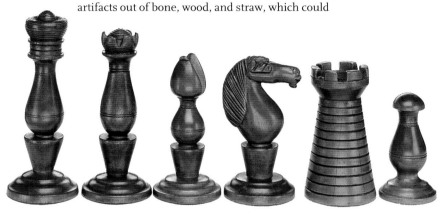

BELOW *Bone "Pulpit" set, one side darkly stained. The place of origin for these sets is not known; although Spain has been suggested there is no supportive corroborative evidence.*

the nineteenth century, including, La Bourdonnais, Staunton, Morphy, Steintz, Blackburn, Zukertort, and Lasker.

be sold in the local marketplace. There is no doubt that the prisoners did include chess sets among their inventory of ship models, spinning jennies, games boxes, and guillotines. The quality of their work varied greatly, from a naïve box of dominoes to superb models of man-of-war galleons.

The few surviving figural chess sets made by prisoners appear to be the work of capable carvers working with unsatisfactory tools. The sets are in the English mode, king, queen, bishops, mounted knights, and rooks carved in the form of

They date stylistically from about 1770 to 1830. No two sets are identical, but all are easy to identify due to their imposing style and the remarkable carving. King 4 inches.

LEFT *Philidor giving a blindfold chess playing exhibition for the Turkish Ambassador at Parsloe's Gentlemen's Club, London, 1793.*

BELOW *Distinctive Irish chessmen made at Killarney from yew or arbutus wood. Often they form part of a set including a folding chess and backgammon board with backgammon-checker pieces to create a compendium of the three games. Both sides of a Killarney Irish set would be turned from the same piece of yew wood, one side being polished darker than the other. With the passage of time the patina of the lighter side tends to darken with the consequence that the differing sides become difficult to distinguish. circa 1800. King 5.5 inches.*

a castle on an elephant, the pawns as pseudo-Roman soldiers. The prisoners must also have made conventional sets of a plain design, but no such chess set, with an undisputed provenance, has been identified.

French Dieppe sets and German Selenus sets have been wrongly attributed in some county museums as Napoleonic prisoner work. It is not possible to be certain where some chess sets were made: mystery surrounds the original source of the "Pulpit" family of sets, for instance. Carved from cattle bone in an original and distinctive style, and indicating a date of between 1770 and 1830, the sets vary in quality from crudely-carved small sets to

ABOVE *Figural "Pulpit" bone set. Very striking and impressive in appearance, but which country or culture does it represent? The answer to this still evades experts. Circa 1800. King 5 inches.*

magnificent, large, half-figural sets. Like the Dieppe and Selenus sets, the Pulpit has also been attributed to prisoners of war.

One of the largest prison camps in England was situated at Normans Cross, near Peterborough, Cambridgeshire. The Peterborough museum has a large collection of artifacts from the Normans Cross camp. There is also a bone Pulpit set at the museum. Unfortunately, this chess set has no corroborative provenance. A local family donated it to the museum in 1953. Pulpit sets do have many features similar to the work of prisoners, but there are also many anomalies—too many to confidently describe the set as a Napoleon prisoner-of-war set. The mystery of where the Pulpit sets may have originated remains for the moment. These sets do have a strong English connection, and perhaps an old colonial one.

The English Potters

Josiah Wedgwood (1730–95) and John Flaxman (1755–1826) are
two of the greatest English potters. Wedgwood, born in the
Staffordshire Potteries area of England, founded his firm in 1759
and within a few years was firmly established as a potter of
distinction and quality. He held strong personal views, being a
humanitarian and supporter of the American struggle for
independence, at a time when these causes were not popular with
his countrymen. Wedgwood, as an admirer of George Washington
and Benjamin Franklin, had Wedgwood jasper medallion portraits
made of them in his factory.

ABOVE *An ivory set,
Romans versus
Saracens, carved by
Robert Carpenter of
Bath, circa 1800.*

Flaxman, born in York, England, was an outstanding artist and sculptor and was commissioned for the first time by Wedgwood in 1775, when only 20. During his lifetime Josiah Wedgwood continued to commission numerous works from Flaxman. They became good friends, even though Wedgwood had written to his manager soon after appointing Flaxman, "I am glad . . . that Flaxman is so valuable an artist. It is but a few years ago since he was a most supreme Coxcombe [exhibitionist] but a little more experience may have cured him of that foible."

Wedgwood, realizing that chess was becoming popular, introduced chess sets as a new line to sell at 5 guineas each, less than the price of ivory sets. He appointed Flaxman to see if a ceramic chess set would be feasible. Flaxman sent Wedgwood a pen and wash drawing of a proposed design in 1783. These were quickly followed by models manufactured at the Wedgwood factory in blue and white jasper. Flaxman's inspiration for the designs came from a mixture of classical and medieval sources. The knight was based on a section of the Parthenon frieze recently brought to England from Greece. The bishop has a genuine Gothic source from Wells Cathedral in southwest England, while the queen is known to have been modeled on the

RIGHT *A selection of Flaxman's original models for the Wedgwood chess set. 1783. At the Sloan Museum, London.*

Shakespearean actress Sarah Siddons as Lady Macbeth, and the king her brother John Phillip Kemble as Macbeth. Flaxman also designed a jester (*fou*) in place of a bishop for sets that were exported to France.

The Staunton Set

Howard Staunton (1810–74) was a Shakespearean scholar and chess champion. The Staunton chess set obtained its name from this remarkable man. In 1843 a chess match, regarded at the time as the equivalent of a world title match, was played in Paris between Staunton and the French champion Pierre de St. Amant. Staunton

ABOVE LEFT *The white queen by artist John Tenniel, from Lewis Carroll's 1887 classic,* Through the Looking Glass.

ABOVE *Tenniel's chess men are used to advertise that it's "Guinness Time".*

ABOVE RIGHT *Ivory Jaques Staunton on ivory and rosewood board.*

BELOW *Zukertort's ivory, red and white Staunton set, with which he played an immortal game against Blackburn, sacrificing his queen to win the game and the tournament in London in 1883. Set made circa 1860. King 4.5 inches.*

decisively won the match, gaining immense national and international fame. He dominated the chess world for the next decade, and his influence prevails in the game today.

The Staunton chessmen were designed by Nathaniel Cook, who registered his drawings under the Ornamental Designs Act, on March 1, 1849. Staunton agreed to endorse the new design. This may have been the first time that a celebrated name was used to promote a commercial product. The sets were made to the highest standard of

craftsmanship by the skilled turners and carvers of John Jaques & Son, sport and games manufacturers, of Hatton Garden, London.

Supported by Staunton's promotion of the set through his regular chess column in the *London Illustrated News*, the new design was an immediate success. Nathaniel Cook, presumably subconsciously, had used prestigious architectural concepts, familiar to an expanding class of educated and prosperous gentry. London architects strongly influenced by Greek and Roman culture were designing prestigious buildings in the neoclassical style. The appearance of the new chessmen was based on this style, and the pieces were symbols of "respectable" Victorian society: a distinguished bishops miter, a queen's coronet and king's crown, a knight carved as a stallion's head from the ancient Greek Elgin Marbles, and a castle streamlined into clean classical lines, projecting an aura of strength and security. The form of the pawns can be seen today in the balconies of London's Victorian buildings. There were also practical innovations: for the first time a crown emblem was stamped onto a rook and knight of each side, to identify their positioning on to the king's side of the board.

LEFT *Howard Staunton, 1810–74. The world's leading chess player in the 1840s. Organized the first modern International Chess Tournament, London 1851. Chess columnist and author, Shakespearian scholar and published in 1864 the complete works of Shakespeare.*

RIGHT *Paul Charles Morphy of New Orleans returned from Europe in 1857 as the uncrowned chess champion of the world, having defeated all the leading chess players of England, France, and Germany. His fame was used by a tobacco company to promote the quality of their product.*

LEFT *The Staunton-St. Amant 1843 historic chess match at the Café de la Régence, Paris. Staunton's decisive victory marked the end of French chess supremacy. For the following half century London became the capital of chess.*

The ebony and boxwood sets were weighted with lead to provide added stability, and the underside of each piece was covered with felt. This afforded the players the illusion that the chessmen were floating across the board.

The Staunton set obtained the stamp of approval of the World Chess Federation when in 1924 it was selected as their choice of set, for use in all future international chess tournaments.

The First Chess Prodigy

Born in New Orleans, Paul Charles Morphy (1837–84) learned to play chess around the age of seven by watching his father and uncle play. He astonished them both one day, by pointing out a combination that they had overlooked. At the age of 12 he amazed everyone by defeating the Hungarian chess master Johann J. Lowenthal, winning all three of their games.

Morphy completed his law studies in 1857, a year early, which allowed him to enter the first American National Chess Congress. This he won in great style, defeating all his opponents. The following year Morphy traveled to Europe, where he again amazed the chess public by winning matches against all the best players in London. In Paris a match was arranged for Morphy to play against Adolf Anderssen of Breslau. Anderssen was regarded as the world's best player. Great public interest was aroused, as this meeting between these two exceptionally talented chess players was being acknowledged as a world championship match. The winner would be the first to win seven games.

RIGHT The 1857 chess match played in Paris between Adolf Anderssen of Germany and America's chess master Paul Morphy in Paris, confirmed Morphy's chess genius, and his status as the world's best player when he won by five clear wins.

LEFT *Four chessmen from a set made to a similar design as the one presented to Morphy. A remarkable and impressive chess set, representing Romans against the Goths. Incorporated onto the rooks is the U.S. national symbol of the American Eagle. Unfortunately, the set has over the course of time been lost. There have been determined efforts to trace it, but all in vain. The same design of set was produced during the second half of the*

ABOVE AND BELOW: *A firm in Millville, New Jersey, produced decorative colorful murrhine glassware at the end of the nineteenth century. Included in their inventory were two designs for chess sets. One was of a set in a conventional style produced in glass, one side made of clear glass*

nineteenth century in Germany by Zimmerman of Hanau. These were manufactured by casting iron in molds, a very specialized technique developed in Germany. By using such a hard metal, a high quality of detail was obtained on the finished models. A set carved in ivory, of the same design as Morphy's, Romans against the Goths, is in the Hermitage Museum, St. Petersburg, Russia.

Anderssen started well, winning the first and drawing the second, then Morphy's genius came to the fore: he won the next four games, and conceding only one further game to Anderssen before winning the match.

Morphy returned to New York to be fêted as a national hero, the first American to obtain world supremacy in any sporting domain. A newspaper account on Morphy's return finished with this statement, "He left the United States the confessed master of American chess, he returned to his native country the champion of the world!"

As a tribute to his outstanding success in defeating the best chess players of Europe, Paul Morphy was presented with a gold and silver chess set and a specially designed gold watch.

opposed by glass of an amber color. The other may also have been based on a conventional design, but the use of clear glass for the basic chessmen and the addition of red and blue glass droplets to indicate the opposing sides has resulted in a pleasantly attractive design.

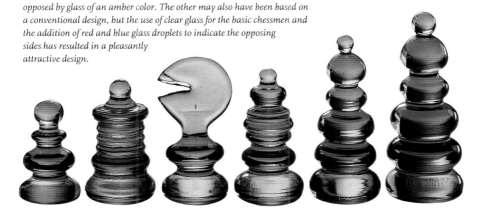

CENTRAL EUROPE

By the nineteenth century, chess sets made for social occasions or for the family home, were available in a choice of designs, provided by many manufacturers. The sets were made from bone, turned and carved into several sections and threaded together.

A king could consist of six or more separate parts assembled by threading onto a central column and polished to

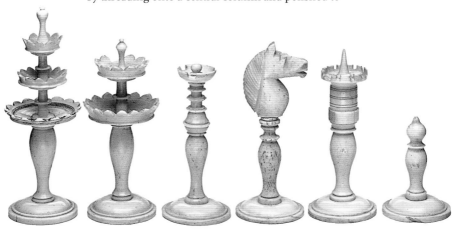

ABOVE AND BELOW *The abstract design of these chess sets corresponds to the formal setting of aristocratic palace gardens, prevalent in Germany and Austria. The chessmen appear to be tranquil by temperament. Fountain-styled kings and queens, of two and three tiers, dominate the central position. Floral bishops stand close by, next to gentle horses. The pawns appear as*

imitate ivory. One side would usually be dyed red, but black and brown were also used. Often the finials could be interchanged to conform with differing customs in West and East Europe, where tradition had the finials of the major pieces in the colors of the opposing side.

The craft of turning was very highly respected in Germany and the turning of a chess set was an important part of an apprentice turner's course. A seal of the Hanover Turners' Guild, established in 1743, displays a chess knight, with a double headed horse as its symbol.

upright flowers to decorate the squares, the whole garden a board, overlooked by the castle towers of a palace building. Chess sets of this genre are known as "Selenus," named after a design illustrated in Gustavus Selenus' Das Schach-oder König-Spiel (Leipzig, 1616). In England these attractive chess sets used to be known as "Tulip sets."

LEFT *German ivory and ebony set following the designs of Micharl Edel, the reknowned turner from Munich, circa 1840. The Edel designs do not have the conventional castle to represent the rook, but bell towers of churches, a familiar sight in the towns of southern Germany. An ivory chess set similar to Edel's designs. The work of a master in the "art of turning." While keeping to the floral motif for the white side, the style of the opposition has been varied with the introduction of ebony sections, with pawns as squared classical balusters and ebony finials. An experienced*

craftsman whose skill is clearly visible in the presentation of his creation.

BELOW LEFT *Another example of an Edel design. Turned, carved and wedged, not threaded, from quality hardwoods, boxwood, and ebony. It is the work of another master of the "art of turning," familiar with Edel's work. Probably these proficient craftsmen were known to each other.*

RIGHT *Edel's line drawings for chess-set design showing the diagonal line touching the top of every piece from king to pawn—a vital element of his designs.*

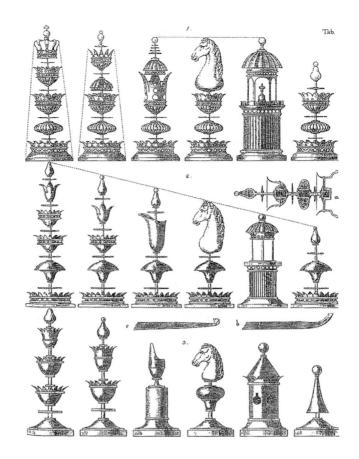

By the nineteenth century, chess had gained the same popularity in the café society of Germany, Austria, and the Netherlands as it had in France, Britain, and the United States; thus—owing to the differing traditions—a much greater variety in the design of chess sets was evident. The most popular pattern, chosen for use in most countries, was the relatively mass-produced French "Régence" set, similar to Benjamin Franklin's. They were exported throughout Europe and are still being used in some remote but long-established cafés that have retained the hospitable ambiance of days gone by.

In southern Germany, Austria, and countries that were a part of or aligned to the Austrian Empire of the Habsburgs, the sets used in the chess clubs and cafés were similar in form to the English sets, although they were generally not so well finished, being turned from soft fruitwood instead of the hardwoods— boxwood, mahogany, or ebony—of the English sets.

Michael Edel, a renowned Munich turner working during the early nineteenth century, published some of his chess-set designs with guidance to turners on their construction.

Edel provided notes with the design: "A chess set of ivory. The construction of the entire set consists of 266 pieces, the threads having equal caliber. Following the old rule, the height of the chess pieces should then, if aligned in one row according to their ranking, decrease in such manner that if one drew a diagonal from the top of the king to the pawn, the tops of all the other pieces must be touched by this line."

A chess set of this design was made for Maximilian Joseph, who had it placed in his famous royal cabinet for ivory carved works made in Munich. The four rooks of this set held a special secret surprise. Within their tower is another miniature chess set, elaborately made from mother-of-pearl and black tortoiseshell.

In the sixteenth century the Habsburg Empire was threatened by the conquering ambitions of Suleiman I (the Magnificent)

BELOW *The contrast between the two cultures of the Habsburgs and the Turks is clearly illustrated in the ivory set pictured here. It has been beautifully crafted with bases and pawns turned in the Edel style, finished with*

(1494–1566), Sultan of the Ottoman Empire. Suleiman expanded the Empire into Hungary, Iran, and Libya. In 1529 Suleiman's ambition to add Austria to his conquests was thwarted at the siege of Vienna by Ferdinand I.

The clash of these two powerful empires was to continue for 175 years. The Austrians called on their Christian allies from Bavaria, Poland, and Hungary, with the blessing of the Pope, to fight crusades against the Muslim heathens, while the Turks fought for the advancement of Islam against the infidels.

The war was continued by Suleiman II against Rodolf II, but it did not reach any conclusion until the third stage, known as the "Great Great Turkish War." In 1688, there was a final and decisive battle. The Ottoman army under Sultan Kara Mustafa had reached the outskirts of Vienna. Leopold and his Christian allies were losing ground to the strength of the invading force, and defeat seemed certain, when, at this crucial moment, a miracle happened for the Christians: reinforcements in the form of the Polish army. Together they decisively defeated the Ottoman forces. With this surrender the Turks were vanquished and driven out of Austria.

This war, with its historical importance to Eastern Europe and to the Habsburgs in particular, has become the natural theme for the design of figural chess sets produced by the craftsmen of the countries of the Austrian Christian Alliance.

The Muhammad Ali, Tyrolean set

During the nineteenth century there developed a school of carving in the Austrian Tyrol to meet the demand of foreign tourists collecting local souvenirs. Among the varied carving subjects of Austrian folk life were traditional chess sets, the most popular theme being the wars between Austria and its ancient and traditional enemy, Turkey.

During the first part of the 1800s Muhammad Ali, an Ottoman general, defeated the Mameluke dynasty of Egypt. His fame was such that the Tyrolean carvers created a chess set to commemorate his achievements. Muhammad Ali was promoted to viceroy of Egypt (1805–49), but he took upon himself the powers of a sultan. With the encouragement of France, Muhammad Ali allowed the ancient culture of Egypt to be exposed and exploited by European curiosity. France in return supported his ambitions. He went to war against his neighbors, conquering the holy cities of Mecca and Medina, and extended the boundaries of Egypt with further conquests of the upper Nile, including raiding Sudan for a limitless supply of slaves. Muhammad Ali's territory eventually extended from Aden in the south, to north along the entire eastern Mediterranean. Muhammad Ali's military success was admired in Europe, and particularly in France, where in Paris a statue has been erected in his honor.

BELOW *The set characterizes the war between Muhammad Ali's Egyptian army and the Sudan, c. 1830. The carving is done in a simplistic professional style, using three differing woods: boxwood for Muhammad's army, ebony and teak for the Sudanese army. The carved chess figures are secured onto rounded stands. On the Egyptian side the king (Muhammad Ali) is*

The Craftsmen of Augsburg

wearing a crown turban, and the pawns wear fezzes. Both sets of bishops appear to be advisers standing with their arms crossed. The four rooks are shaped as mosques while the queens on either side wear loose clothing and have coronets on their heads. The Sudanese king also wears a coronet, while the Sudanese pawns are shown wearing feathered headgear.

RIGHT *An elephant rook from the famous German Augsberg designers.*

Over the centuries, German carvers and sculptors had developed a distinctive and creative method for producing exquisite works of art in an exaggerated and animated form. The sculptured works of the best German craftsmen have rarely been equaled. Towns such as Augsburg and Nuremberg obtained enviable reputations for the high quality of their crafts and artistic products.

An impressive example of the high standard achieved and produced by Augsburg craftsmen can be seen in a chess set and board made in 1735. It combines the skills of many craftsmen: the silversmith, Christian Baur, whose silver mark is displayed on the stepped silver bases of the chessmen; the master of inlay, for the tortoiseshell and

ABOVE *This set continues a traditional theme inspired by a chess morality, written in 1300 by a Dominican friar, Jacobus de Cessolis, entitled* The Customs of Men and the Duties of Nobles. *De Cessolis uses chess as a parable for society, defining the duties of the royals and nobles to their subjects, the pawns. The pawns are characterized as people in differing trades and occupations. In his morality he chose a laborer, a woodsman, a physician, a magistrate, a chemist, an innkeeper, a constable, and a villain. These were the original de Cessolis pawns. Carvers in southern Germany maintained this motif when*

creating figural chess sets, although, as can be seen here, the occupations varied. The pawns on one side represent farm hands, each one handling a different farm implement. The opposing pawns are peasants carrying out various activities. The bishops hold staffs to represent magistrates, while the knights are runners or messengers. Vida's elephant and castle, as the rooks, are by this period well established in decorative sets. The chess set works well as a magnificent work of art, but, as a players' set, it could be frustrating to play a game because of the difficulty in distinguishing between the law (bishops) and the runners (knights).

mother-of-pearl squares on the chessboard veneered in tortoiseshell and ebony; the cabinet maker for the board made as a coffer to hold the chessmen; and the master carver to make the chessmen. Together they create a chess set that is a work of high art and sublimely attractive.

BELOW *Turned from fruitwood the design of the chessmen follows the tradition of the earlier turners by creating the pawn, bishop, queen, and king to the same basic shape primarily distinguished by their varying sizes. The rook is fashioned in the form of a castle tower,*

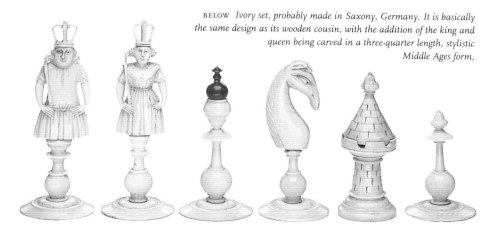

BELOW *Ivory set, probably made in Saxony, Germany. It is basically the same design as its wooden cousin, with the addition of the king and queen being carved in a three-quarter length, stylistic Middle Ages form,*

Dutch, Danish, or Deutsch?

as built in central Europe, finished with a high cone-shaped roof. The knight is carved as a stylized horse's head. The opposing sides would normally be dyed brown against black and completed with finials of ivory opposed by ebony. Circa 1830. King 4.5 inches.

Northern Europe had a distinctive conventional and attractive design of chess set, which originated in the eighteenth century and continued in practical use until the second half of the nineteenth century. It appears to have been a pattern used by different manufacturers in different countries. That is why the question arises: Is it Dutch, Danish, or German?

both holding a scepter as a symbol of their sovereignty. One side is dyed red, except for the bishops' finials, which have been exchanged in accordance with the custom for Eastern Europe. Circa 1810. King 3.5 inches.

The same basic design was also used for ivory sets: they, too, come in at least two variants of the same style. One uses red coloring to indicate the different sides, while the other is in white against brown. These sets are turned, except for the carved king, queen, and knights. The monarchs are simply carved, in a medieval style wearing high crowns, which is an indication that they are probably of German origin.

BELOW *A wooden conventional set of Eastern Europe. Turned from fruitwood, one side varnished a light brown against black. The king and queen have the fountain appearance of the German bone sets, the bishops wear reverse-color hats,*

the rook is shaped as a tower, and the knight is simply carved in a stylized form. The Polish artist Jan Matejko owned such a set. It is now housed in the Matejko Museum, Cracow. Circa 1890. King 3.5 inches.

"Chess and vodka
are born brothers."
—*Russian proverb*

Chess arrived in Russia by the direct trading routes from northern India and Iran. There is no exact date for this but, by the end of the first millennium the state of Russia was emerging by uniting with many of the eastern Slavic nations. There was no Russian literature referring to chess until the thirteenth century, possibly due to a negative attitude held by the church, which placed chess with gambling, dice, and other "devilish delusions."

However, in Russian folklore and ancient ballads, chess is often mentioned. One ballad recalls how, at the tenth-century court of Prince Vladimir of Kiev, chess tournaments were part of regular festivities, as well as entertainment for visiting foreign envoys. The abundance of chessmen found in archaeological excavations throughout Russia, from the tenth to thirteenth centuries, provides ample evidence that the game was being played in Russia by the tenth century. Even the earliest, eighth-century chessmen, excavated at Afrasiab, Samarqand, are from a southern territory of the Soviet Union. In the northern town of Novgorod, ancient chess pieces found in excavations provide good examples of the style of Russian abstract pieces from the twelfth century through to the fifteenth century.

Novgorod was established in the tenth century as a trading center on the Volkhov river. By the fifteenth century it had prospered to become one of the most important towns in Russia, with a population of over 50,000. Extensive archaeological excavations took place in the ancient part of Great Novgorod during the middle of the last century. A profusion of artifacts were unearthed, and in one particular dig more that 20,000 objects were discovered, among them some 50 chess pieces.

The basic design of these chessmen is recognized as being related to the abstract form of the Arabic chess pieces being used

ABOVE AND PREVIOUS PAGE *Russian carvers in Kholmogory, a village near Archangel, were carving figural sets to a standard design from the seventeenth century. The set is based on the continuous wars against the Turks of the Ottoman Empire over territorial rights to Russia's southern borders. The rook on the Russian side has a double-masted man-of-war opposed by a Turkish single-masted galleon. Both sides have mounted soldiers as knights. Indian elephants represent the bishops, the Russian elephant has an advantage of having a mounted mahout. A Russian czar seated on a throne is opposed by a Turkish sultan, both have a ferz or counsellor at their side. The Russian pawns are in Graeco-Roman style uniforms, the Turks dressed in Muslim fashion and turbans.*

in Europe during the same medieval period. With the Novgorod chess finds there appears to be some design differences, because these pieces are cut from wood instead of ivory or bone. The survival of so many wood chessmen was apparently due to the Novgorod earth being exceptionally dry. Surprisingly, the chessmen are remarkably small, averaging only one inch, making the pawns very small indeed. The pieces are crudely carved, probably because chess was played by the general populace, who made sets by whittling wood. The king and queen, the largest pieces, are plain small pieces of wood cut in the round with roundel finials. They represent a czar and a ferz (vizier), in the Persian tradition.

ABOVE *Reproduction of the fifteenth-century chessmen excavated in Russia. This is one of the earliest designs for turned chess pieces. From the left: a bishop with the cleft top, a ferz or queen, shaped as a vase, a czar in three tiers, a pawn, a small version of the czar, a knight well stylized, and a rook, boat-shaped on a base.*

The bishop piece has two ridged protrusions to indicate the tusks of an elephant, which it is meant to portray the same as in the original Indian *chaturanga* (chess). The knight, as in early Arabic and European pieces, has a triangle protrusion to indicate a horse head. The castle has a V cleft cut into the upper part of the piece, similar to the early Arabic rook. But in Russia this shape is not meant to be a chariot but a boat (a *ladia*). The pawns are neatly cut pieces of wood to represent foot soldiers, the Russian name is *peshka*.

It is intriguing that, although there was a vast distance and conflicting cultures between Russia and Europe, the Islamic style of stocky carved chessmen was to lose favor in both cultures during the fourteenth and fifteenth centuries.

The main cause for the change seems to be the development in the progress of lathe technology, and improvements in the tools used by turners for cutting ivory and bone. The Russian chess set turners established their own distinctive form. The king and queen, or czar and ferz, were turned to differing patterns, the czar in three tiers, the ferz as a vase-shaped cylinder. The rook began to appear as a boat on a pedestal. The bishop was upright but with a cut down the center, maintaining the symbol of the elephant tusks. The knight, turned and carved, was pleasantly stylized. The pawn was dignified by being turned to a similar shape to the czar, but with only one tier.

THE ROYAL RUSSIAN COURT

The czars of Russia loved their chess. Ivan the Terrible died while playing a game and another czar ordered that chess was the only game to be played by the royal family and at the royal court.

Czar Alexei Mikhailovich, when only seven years old, was bought a wooden chess set and board from a local market by his father, Mikhail Fedorovich. The game became a lifelong passion for Alexei, to the extent that he ordered ivory carvers of Kholmogory, the *shakmatchiki*, to be brought to the court in Moscow, solely to create chess sets and boards for him.

In 1675, Joachim Skultet, Ambassador of Brandenburg, brought a gift of a silver chess set and table for Czar Mikhailovich. This set has survived to the present day, and is an excellent example of the high quality of the jeweler's art of the period. The chess pieces are figural, all presented as if moving: a soldier with a club, a rearing horse with rider, an elephant with a mahout (driver), a king in armor, a queen, and the pawns as musketeers.

Peter the Great, the son of Alexei Mikhailovich, inherited his father's passion for chess. Czar Peter would play against his generals on their many campaigns against the Turks. He taught his son Alexei to play, considering it to be an important part of his education. There is a record that in 1697 the Czar ordered for his son Alexei a chessboard painted in gold, "in size one *arshin* [2 feet 8 inches wide], of good workmanship." Czar Peter also

BELOW *The Kholmogory chess men, characterizing Russia against Turkey. The Turkish side is dyed black, but red was also used to distinguish the different armies. Peter the Great came to England in the 1670s to study how to make western European warships. It appears that this is the design of ship that the Kholmogory carvers have used as a model for their chess sets. Circa 1800. King 3.5 inches.*

ABOVE *Czar Ivan the Terrible (1530–84), portrayed on his deathbed playing his last game of chess.*

encouraged the game to be played at his court, by his officials, his generals, and the nobility.

Catherine the Great continued the chess tradition of the czars, and one of her regular playing partners was General Prince Potyomkin Tavrichesky. It was said of him, "With one hand he plays chess, while with the other he conquers his enemies."

A Rome ambassador to Moscow (1670–73), writing about the royal children, stated, "The Russians do not at all permit dancing,

fist fights, and other noble exercises that are widespread among us. They play so-called chess, the famous Persian game, a truly royal game by its name and nature. They play daily, and they develop their intellect to a surprising degree."

In the nineteenth century, Czar Pavel I, before he was crowned, traveled incognito around Europe. Under the pseudonym of "the Northern Count" he played chess at every opportunity, and made a point of visiting the chess cafés of Vienna and Paris to match his skill against their best players.

Czar Nikolai II promoted international chess, funding the Chigorin Memorial in 1909. Chigorin was the first Russian chess player to challenge for the world title, losing in 1889 to Steinitz. Czar Nikolai also funded the prestigious St.Petersburg Tournament, where the term "grandmaster" was first introduced to describe outstanding chess players.

In the Central State Archive of Ancient Documents, Moscow, there is an order, written in 1670, from Czar Alexei Mikhailovich Romanov. It is a requisition to Kholmogory for 10 chess sets and 10 combs. Unfortunately, there was a fire in the carver's workshop that destroyed most of the ivory so they were able to complete only seven sets. This was reported to the Czar by his agents: "And there have been given, Sire, for these seven sets of chess, for the ivory and for the workmanship, six rubles, nineteen *altyny*, three *dengi*. And these seven sets of chess are sent to thee, Great Ruler-Czar and Grand Prince Alexei Mikhailovich of all Greater and Lesser and White Russia Autocrat to Moscow by us, thy servants, under seal."

Portrait of Czarina Catherine II (1729–96), Empress of Russia from 1762 also known as Catherine the Great. Despite the length of her rule she is popularly most remembered for the many lovers she took during her reign.

Catherine the Great

Catherine the Great, had a special chess set presented to her by the workers of the Tula Arms Factory. The factory, which was founded in 1712, became the center of Russian arms production. During the war against Sweden the armory craftsmen had to work to annual production quotas of 15,000 flintlock rifles with bayonets for dragoons and soldiers. In times of peace the craftsmen were allowed special privileges such as buying iron at discount prices to make their own artifacts, which they were able to sell without paying duty to the state.

Czarina Catherine II frequently ordered richly decorated hunting weapons from the Tula factory to present as gifts to visiting foreign dignitaries. In 1782 plans were submitted to the Czarina for the construction of a new Tula arms factory. Catherine approved and signed the plans but did not authorize any payment to enable the work to commence. The Tula craftsmen, knowing of her fondness for chess, decided to remind her of their project by creating a chess set worthy of an Empress and presenting it to her.

The set was encased in a steel casket with decorations in applied bronze. Engraved on the lid and the sides of the casket was an illustration of the proposed new arms factory. An inventory at the Hermitage Museum, St. Petersburg, written in 1786, describes the gift as, "A box, square, steel with a lid, gilded in places. Its inside is lined with crimson velvet and there are places made for chess pieces of which there are eighty in number."

Since then 32 of the chessmen have gone missing. Could someone have taken them to play a game, and forgotten to return them? The chess pieces are made of steel and decorated with bronze and silver gilding. The opposing sides are silver against gold. The technique of die stamping was unknown at the time, so each chess piece had to be made by hand from many separately forged parts, joined and skillfully fixed around a central dowel with

BELOW A steel knight, decorated with inlays of bronze and silver gilding, one of the chessmen made in 1785 for Catherine the Great, by Adreian Sukhnov, a master craftsmen at Tula's arms factory.

decorative details being inlayed into the individual pieces. The creation of this wonderful gift for Czarina Catherine is attributed to Tula's master craftsman, Adreian Sukhnov. Unfortunately for the armory craftsmen of Tula, their diplomatic scheme did not work sufficiently to persuade the Empress to provide the necessary funds for the building of their new factory.

BELOW *Conventional playing set in brown and white bone from North Russia. Similar sets were also turned from wood. The eighteenth-century design follows the pattern of the other early turned playing sets,*

BELOW *Chessmen from a "Little Faces" set. Turned and carved from walrus ivory. An old manuscript describes a similar designed set as being made from mammoth bone, made in Archangel. At the Hermitage there is another set dated to the eighteenth century.*

Little Faces

Russia also has a tradition of sets they describe as "with little faces." This can apply to their full figural carved sets, but normally this expression describes Russian conventional playing sets, finished with carved heads. The majority of these sets that are

with the pawn, bishop, queen, and king being similar except for size, a stylized carved horse head for the knight and the boat beginning to resemble the castle or tower of western European sets. Circa 1800. King 3 inches.

As with the plain bone set, the forms of the pawn, bishop, queen, and king are basically the same except for height. The set also boasts an attractive carved knight and the ladia or boat, shaped like a river fisherman's coracle with a central mast. Circa 1800. King 3 inches.

extant come from Kholmogory, carved from bone or walrus ivory. The design has a lot of natural charm, and surprisingly, while very few of these sets are of the same pattern, their family roots are easily recognized. Their rook/*ladia* is a round tub shape with a central mast; the knights tend to vary, but are always distinctive and adorable; the bishops, royals, and pawns all have the "little faces." These sets are meant to be played with and are developed from the eighteenth-century standard Russian set.

To Revolution and beyond

In 1760 the Imperial Porcelain Factory in St. Petersburg produced one of the earliest chess sets to be made in porcelain. From the half-dozen remaining pieces, which can be seen at the Hermitage Museum, the set must have been very attractive and colorful. The theme is the traditional Russians-against-Turks. The pieces that have survived are two pawns (one Russian and one Turk), a rook as a *ladia* (a small rowing boat carrying two Russian women; unfortunately, one has lost her head), a queen, or possibly the sultana (sitting cross-legged on a cushion throne), a knight (as a white horse standing upright on all fours), and the bishop (as an elephant being ridden by a mahout). Pawns are placed on plinths and the major chess pieces are placed on pedestal stands.

After the October Revolution in 1916, art and chess were initially encouraged by the communist government, and used to propagate their new ideals and political system to the soviet people and to other nations. The Lomonosov Porcelain Factory made a number of striking chess sets designed by the sculptress Natalia Danko and her sister, the artist Yelena. They produced a "proletarian style" for chess sets which complemented the prevailing fashion for Art Deco in the United States and Europe. One of their sets, entitled "Town and Country," has factories and industry on one side, opposed by fruit and corn. The pieces have been created in an attractive, colorful, surreal form.

The sisters' most successful design was named by the Dandos as the "Reds and Whites." This set is of interest in the West for its propagandist subject matter: capitalists against workers. It is also admired as a set of notable artistic merit. The styles of the chessmen harmonize as a complete entity, unified by the strong colors obtained from the quality porcelain created in the manufacturing process. The well-made chessmen depict on one side the reds—workers liberated from industrial slavery, presented as happy and strong. Facing them are the whites—greedy capitalists, their workers kept in chains, controlled by a king who is the embodiment of corruption and death. Faced with such a choice, who would choose capitalism?

This set was originally made in 1922; it was out of production from 1939 owing to the outbreak of World War II and then the isolation that followed during the Cold War.

Since the end of the Cold War further productions of the Red and White sets have been made to a limited degree. The outward appearance of these later sets is the same as the originals; only the weight differs. The later chess sets are not produced in the solid form of the earlier ones.

ABOVE *Count Leo Tolstoy, the author of* War and Peace *was an avid chess player. Here he is seen playing against his friend Michail Sukotin, surrounded by his family. When Tolstoy was an officer in the Caucasus, he was caught playing chess when on duty. As punishment he was confined to barracks on the day his unit were awarded medals for gallantry, so he never obtained the medal. Tolstoy's chess table and his English Jaques–Staunton set of boxwood and ebony are kept at the Tolstoy State Museum, Moscow.*

Tis all a Chequer-board of Nights and Days
Where Destiny with Men for Pieces plays:
Hither and thither moves, and mates, and slays,
And one by one back in the Closet lays.
—*Rubaiyat of Omar Khayyam. c. 1000*

By the fifteenth century, Islam, and therefore Islamic art, had spread within the vast Muslim empire from the Atlantic shores of North Africa to the boundaries of southern China. Within this complex empire were absorbed the many varying cultures and religions of Asia. In general, the Islamic conquerors allowed the established religions within their territory to continue without overt persecution for their faithful.

Christians, Hindus, and Buddhists were allowed to conduct their religions in peace. The artists and craftsmen were also allowed to continue their occupation and to develop their skills in accordance with their cultural, political, and aesthetic traditions.

The Islamic chessmen of the tenth century maintained their same basic shape for centuries, altering only gradually. By the thirteenth century the chessmen were being turned but remained the same size, the upper protrusions were still carved, to distinguish the elephant from the horse. The shah and firzan differed only in size, the shah being the larger. The rook has a turned base topped by the conventional carved-V, cleft-shape finish. The pawns are turned as a smaller version of the shah.

By the sixteenth century all the chess pieces are being turned, probably on bow lathes. The Ashmolean Museum in Oxford, England, had ivory chessmen from Egypt, which have been radiocarbon dated. They were found to range in date from 1470 to 1650.

ABOVE AND PREVIOUS PAGE *Ancient Burmese chessmen carved in the Buddhist traditional style from local ivory. The Mingyi, or Great King, in the center carries a spear in his right hand and a staff of office in his left hand. Originally these ivory chessmen had been colored maroon and black. The favored colors for Burmese chess sets.*

LEFT *Egyptian ivory chessmen, similar to ones at the Ashmolean Museum. From the left: bishop, bishop, rook, king, rook, knight. Both sides are made to the same pattern, distinguished by coral stone decoration opposed by jet stones. Circa seventeenth century.
King 1.5 inches.*

WELLED SELLASSE, RAS OF TIGRE

In 1805, Henry Salt, secretary to Lord Valentia, was sent to Ethiopia on an exploratory mission. There he discovered a well-ordered society ruled by Welled Sellasse, the Ras of Tigre. He recalled that, on his arrival at Antalow, he and his guides were invited to join the Ras at breakfast. In the evening they went to the hall, where the Ras was playing chess with his chiefs. Salt describes the chessmen as "coarsely made of ivory, are very large and clumsy."

I observed that their game differs from ours. Bishops jump over the heads of knights, and are only allowed to move three squares. The pawns move only one step at starting, and get no rank by reaching the end of the board. When the players have occasion to take any one of their adversary's pieces, they strike it with great force and eagerness from its place. They play with much noise; every person around, even the slaves, having a voice in the game, and seizing the pieces at pleasure to show any advisable move. We observed, however, that they always managed with great ingenuity to let the Ras win every game.

Salt was describing the rules for the old *shatranj* form of chess, the Muslim rules not having been changed since the seventh century. The Ras certainly had discovered how to have great fun playing the game.

INDIA

It is generally recognized that chess originated in India in or around the sixth century A.D. Surprisingly, although figural chessmen from the seventh to eighth centuries have been excavated to the north of India in Samarqand and tenth-century conventional Islamic pieces from neighboring Iran, there is no archaeological evidence of early chessmen being found in India. Possibly the earliest two known Indian chessmen are at

LEFT *Rama and his wife Sita, the scene shows them enjoying a game of chess. Rama is the hero of the epic poem, Ramayana. It tells of how he defeated the evil demon king, Ravana. He is worshiped as the ideal human, brave, handsome, loyal, and kind, a good husband, and a fair king.*

ABOVE *A Muslim design turned from ivory, one side colored red, the other green, the normal colors for Indian sets. These chessmen resemble a set shown in Hyde 1694, which came from Surat. They have the unusual feature of being hollow, and within each piece are threads of silver tin, which allow the piece to be rung like a bell when moved.*

RIGHT *A chess knight, similar to the one shown here and possibly from the same original set, is at the Victoria and Albert Museum, London. The museum attributes the piece to the Hindu kingdom of Vijayanagar in southern India and dates it to the late sixteenth century. The carving is typical of that used for Hindu deities in Indian temples.*

BELOW *Early nineteenth-century Rajasthan chessmen, carved in a tradition and style that had been continuous for hundreds of years. The carving is naïve but attractive. The set's size is impressive, and the pieces are precisely polychromed in green and gold with red trim, opposed to white and gold with red trim. Circa 1840. King 6 inches.*

the Victoria and Albert Museum in London. An elephant and a knight, they may even be from the same set. They have been attributed to the Hindu state of Vijayanagar, and dated to the latter part of the sixteenth century. There is a part Rajasthan set at the Staatliche Kunstsammlungen, Historisches Museum, Dresden. Were it not for an irrefutable provenance provided by the records of the museum, which accurately date these 25 chessmen to the year 1610, it would have been assumed that they were made in the nineteenth century. The most obvious difference between the 1610 pieces and Rajasthan sets from the nineteenth century are their size, the earlier chessmen being much smaller and more delicate than the later ones. However, there are some other indications that testify to their seventeenth-century date, namely in the contemporary fashion of uniforms being worn by the pawns and the horses' body armor of the early set.

ABOVE *A comparison in size of two small Rajasthan chessmen from the seventeenth century, a knight with horse and the elephant king with raised trunk, against a nineteenth-century Rajasthan king carrying cannons.*

RIGHT *A selection of Muslim-designed chessmen. From the left: king, ivory queen, king, ivory king, rook, horn king and two pawns in front.*

Thomas Hyde, *Professor of Hebrew and Arabic at Queen's College, Oxford.*

Thomas Hyde had published in 1694 *De Ludis Orientalibus*, a history of oriental games including chess, the so-called "royal game." His was the first book to seriously investigate the origins of chess, which he correctly attributed to northwest India. In his treatise he provides drawings of Hindu figural chess pieces of carved ivory and three examples of Muslim chess pieces from sets acquired in Bombay and presented as a gift to Hyde by Sir D. Sheldon: one was turned from wood, and had a board; the second was turned from solid ivory, and varnished; the third ivory set was turned, hollowed, and pierced; and within each piece were placed strands of Indian silver. One side was stained red the other green. When a player moved such a chess piece he could ring it like a bell.

There is little change in the design of the seventeenth-century Hyde chessmen, which came from Surat, and the Muslim chess

ABOVE *A colorful scene of two Persians relaxing by enjoying a game of chess and a shared water pipe smoke.*

LEFT *Another view of the colorful wooden Muslim set featured below. Despite its gaudiness, the paint is so striking and glossy it provides the set with a certain panache rarely seen in chess sets.*

BELOW *A turned wood, Indian Muslim set with ivory finials. The colors red and green have been mixed in a mottled pattern, one side dominated*

BELOW *A colorful Muslim chess set painted in the unusual colors of purple against orange. The king and queen are much larger than one might expect from an Indian set*

sets made during the following centuries; and even in this millennium Islamic craftsmen continue to produce sets to the same traditional pattern. It is interesting to observe that these later chessmen are designed to complement the architecture of Muslim culture, the pieces turned in a style that resembles the mosques and minarets of Islam.

Warren Hastings (1732–1818)

Governor of Bengal, Warren Hastings had previously been an official of the East India Company. As governor, he initiated many changes, improving the legal and fiscal systems of British India. The authority and status he obtained through these changes upset some very influential Members of Parliament. They brought him

by red opposed by a dominant green. The pattern corresponds with similar sets from Lahore in the Punjab. Circa 1870. King 2.5 inches.

and the colors are not traditional. The set is probably early twentieth century and may have been made to appeal to foreign tourists. Circa 1930. King 4 inches.

to trial for the vague crime of alleged misconduct. The trial lasted for seven years before he was acquitted of all charges.

During Hastings's period as governor, there was a rapid growth in the influx of English gentry to Bengal. One such was a judge, Sir William Jones, author of an essay, "The Indian Game of Chess." At the age of 17 he wrote the poem "Cassia," whose heroine has became the chess players' "Muse of Chess."

BELOW A set made in India, possibly in Vizagapatam, for the European market. The design is based on eighteenth-century English ivory sets that were introduced to Indian carvers. They transformed them into

BELOW Another example of a set based on an old English style, reproduced in India and transformed into an exotic creation. A nineteenth-century report in India referred to a set of this form as "a handsome set of chessmen, which although carved in India (Jaipur), are Chinese in manner and

this more attractive decorative set, which is a practical design and would please any chess player. Turned and delicately carved from ivory one side colored a reddish orange. Circa 1850. King 4.5 inches.

Chess was a popular pastime among the English and it was around this time that an ivory carving industry became established at Murshidabad, capital of Bengal, to cater to the tastes of the expanding British community. Among the many artifacts produced were chess sets. A typical set carved at Murshidabad has a provenance associating it to the Hastings family. The set provides an excellent example of the style and quality achieved by

seem to be imitated". The Chinese set referred to is also based on the same English design, with the exception of the pawns which have original carved heads. Normally these Anglo-Indian sets are colored white and red, but occasionally, as with this set, the Indian colors of red and green are used. Circa 1850. King 5 inches.

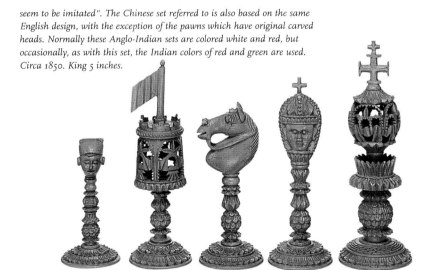

the Hindu carvers and the high standard of the polychrome finish obtained by the artists. They were clearly using the favored Indian colors for chess, green, red, and gold, to produce a very striking and impressive chess set.

A few miles outside Murshidabad the British built an army barrack town at Berhampur, where another carving center was established to provide quality souvenirs for visiting dignitaries, officers, their wives, and the soldiers. Among the chess sets made at Berhampur, the "John" chess sets, carved from ivory, were superbly designed. They represented, on one side, the mercenary

BELOW Carved ivory Murshidabad polychrome set representing a mogul army, probably that of a Nawab of Bengal, whose seat of government was at Murshidabad. There is no European influence in the design of this set. The king, queen,

BELOW *Usually turned from ivory and horn, this Visagapatam form of set was also made from sandalwood and ivory. Sometimes it was part of an impressive compendium with backgammon and checkers manufactured with an inlaid box board made from ivory, sandalwood, and ebony, containing three ivory boxes to hold the chessmen and counters, also made from ivory and horn.*

and bishops are represented riding elephants, the knights are mounted soldiers and the rooks are camels with riders, all correctly conforming with a mogul Indian army of the eighteenth century. Circa 1800. King 4 inches.

army of the East India Company, and on the other, an Indian state army led by a maharaja. The name "John" derived from the common name being used for the East India Co.

The standard of the carving matched that of Murshidabad, but the John sets were not painted, the ivory being left natural; only the bases of one side were stained brown. Sets from these centers could also be made to special order. An example of such a set is in the Indian Collection of the Victoria and Albert Museum. It portrays Muslims against Hindus; it is exceptionally well carved and very impressive.

The London firm of Lund, who catered to the gentry, were so impressed with this Indian compendium that they made their own version out of ebony and ivory, one side of the chess set and half the counters dyed red. Their chess set was almost identical to the basic design of the Anglo-Indian set, which had itself been based on an English eighteenth-century set.

In the late eighteenth century elaborate ornamental lathes were invented and manufactured by Holtzapffel for use by the European gentry. They were highly popular and examples of the eccentric ivory artifices that were produced on a Holtzapffel lathe can been seen in a corridor cabinet at the Rosenborg Palace, Copenhagen. The lathe could be programmed to create the most elaborate geometric shapes with engineering precision. Chess sets were made by this process, although there is no evidence that they were manufactured on a commercial basis. However, in 1824, a Jacob Petit published in London drawings of objects, that included chess sets, which he recommended as suitable to be made on ornamental lathes. These modest line sketches appear to have been the inspiration for the Indian turner-carvers of Berhampur in the creation of a distinctive Victorian design for turned ivory sets. It is ironic that these sets were turned by accomplished craftsmen working on primitive bow lathes, and not as intended on an ornamental lathe by gentlemen indulging in one of their hobbies.

Vizagapatam

The British East India Company, set up in 1600 to trade in Asian spices, at its height controlled a quarter of world trade. It was an amazingly successful commercial company, and with its own army, won political power in India. The company established a craft manufacturing center in Vizagapatam (sometimes spelled Vizagapatnam) at the end of the seventeenth century. The local native workers specialized in quality products appropriate for export, by the company, to the colonies of the British Empire, North America, and Europe.

There seem to have been a number of chess workshops in Vizagapatam, producing differing styles of conventional turned sets, but based on English eighteenth-century designs.

BELOW Anglo-Indian Vizagapatam rook, in the shape of a castle tower with flag pole, turned from ivory, circa 1840.

ABOVE AND BELOW
*Beautifully carved
ivory chessmen from
Berhampur. A set
depicting Hindus and
Moslems, now housed
in the reserve
collection of the
Victoria and Albert
Museum, London.
Circa 1850.*

The Pepys set

One very attractive design imported is normally referred to as a
"Pepys" set. Such a set, with a box board and backgammon
counters, was presented to the London Museum by the Pepys
Cockerell family, descendants of the diarist Samuel Pepys. They
believed that it had been a gift from King James II, which, if
correct, would date the set to around 1680. The board appears to
be of the right craftsmanship for this period, which does provide
some credence to the story, but the ivory set can be compared with
similar sets at the Victoria and Albert Museum which are recorded
as being from Vizagapatam no earlier than the turn of the

nineteenth century. It is probable that this impressive set was added to the board at the later date by a member of the family visiting or working in India.

The sets made for export for the East India Company and those made to cater for English taste did to a certain extent modify

BELOW *The '"Pepys" set. One of the most impressive designs for an Anglo-Indian set that has evolved to become more decorative and artistic than conventional. Expertly turned and carved from ivory, with one side always dyed an attractive Indian green. Circa 1820. King 6 inches.*

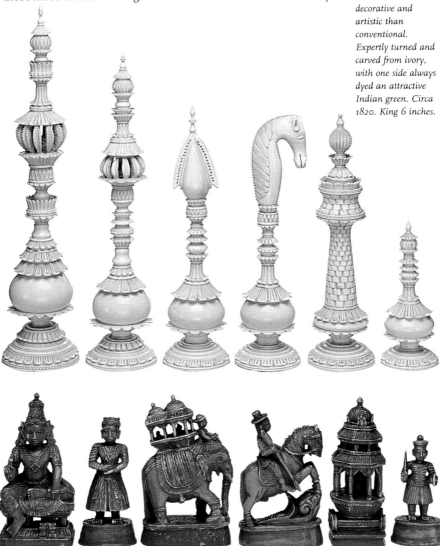

the style of carving of the traditional Hindu Indian artist. They would carve in the inherited style used over centuries by masons whose sculptured masterpieces of their varied gods impressively adorn the ancient Hindu and Buddhist temples built throughout the subcontinent.

The Sikhs

The Sikhs, unlike the Hindus, believe in only one god: the opening words of their sacred text, the Guru Granth Sahib, states, "There is one supreme eternal reality; the truth; immanent in all things; creator of all things; immanent in creation." This may explain why they were able to empathize with the Christian British Raj. They gained an enviable reputation as soldiers fighting against the Muslim tribesmen of Afghanistan during the nineteenth century and, in the twentieth, fought with the British in Burma to save India from the Japanese invaders.

The Sikhs' home state, Punjab, is in northern India, where they have always been aware of the threat from China, historically their natural enemies. This constant anxiety within the Sikh nation is manifest in the theme chosen by a Sikh carver for an ivory chess set. It represents the war of their nightmares on the 64-squared battlefield. The Sikh army, carved in green, armed only with their symbolic "kirpan" swords, have to face the Chinese armed with muskets from a past era. The major pieces portray the traditional symbols of an Indian army, carved heads of a camel, a horse, and an elephant, although the kings and queens in this set seem to be the equivalent to a general and his adjutant, rather than royals.

BURMA

Buddhism originated in the sixth century B.C. in northern India. The Buddha, Siddhartha Gautama, was brought up in luxury, a prince destined to be king. He rejected this life of comfort and power and dedicated himself to finding an answer to all the suffering he saw within his community. Meditating under a bodhi tree (a fig tree), he received "the Great Enlightenment" and became Buddha, meaning, "the enlightened one." The Buddhist religion spread east and south to embody China and Burma.

The Buddhists, having evolved from the Hindu culture, share many of the same legends and their temples are built in a similar architectural style, including the extensive and beautifully elaborate exterior carving.

Chess in Burma is called *sittuyin*, meaning the representation of an army. The major pieces translate to: great king, general, elephant, horse, and chariot. But in their sets the chariot has been changed to a temple, and the horse and elephant

LEFT *A set carved to represent the great victory of Hanuman's monkeys—here mounted on an elephant and a horse—over Ravana's dreaded demons.*

BELOW *An excellent example of the best of Buddhist carving, this set is made in a stylistic form that belongs only to the craftsmen of Burma, and can be seen in the architecture of the Buddhist temples. Circa 1800. King 4 inches.*

usually have riders. Often the riders and the pawns are carved as monkeys, to honor the legend of Rama (told in the Ramayana), when the monkeys, led by their general-king, Hanuman, defeated Ravana, the ten-headed king of the demons.

RIGHT *Frank Sinatra in the film* Tony Rome *admires an ivory carved Chinese chess set.*

Most Burmese sets are carved from wood and painted black and red; the carving tends to be naive but in a conventional style. The ivory sets, with one side normally colored maroon, are usually well carved, conforming to the same conventional pattern. These Burmese sets are all carved as actual figures: there is no simplified turned version on offer as a compromise to the convenience of chess players.

MONGOLIA

ABOVE *A cart is a traditional representation for a Mongolian rook. It is often simplified and depicted as a wheel, but can be elaborated on to be any form that denotes movement.*

The great Mongolian emperor Tamerlane (or Timur Lang, meaning "Timur the Lame") (1336–1405) ruled over a vast empire extending from China to India, where his descendants were to establish the Mogul dynasty that would last well into the nineteenth century. Tamerlane was a famed warrior who was known to have as great a passion for his chess army, as he did for his real warfare. He named one of his sons "Shah-rukh" (Check-rook), and a newly built town, "Shahrukhiya" (Checkrookcity). It occurred because he was playing a game of chess with one of his commanders when he was interrupted by two messengers arriving together, one with the news that his new city had been finished and the other with the news that his concubine had given birth to a son. Tamerlane had just completed a chess move, giving check with his rook, which completely destroyed his opponent's game. Tamerlane was so excited and happy in finding such a strong move at the same moment he received such good news that he celebrated by naming his son and the town after the chess move in memory of such a fortuitous moment.

There were a number of skilled chess players in Tamerlane's court, the most renowned being Ali Aladdin at-Tabrizi. He said that he had had a dream in which he had received his skill, in a bag with a chess set. Since when, no one had beaten him or could beat

him. He certainly seems to have been a very gifted player, according to accounts of his play: he moved quickly, never appearing to think studiously over his moves. He would often play against more than one player at a time, even playing blindfold chess against two opponents simultaneously. When he played Tamerlane, they would play "Great Chess," chess on a board 12 x 12 square. The results of their games are not recorded but Tamerlane is believed to have said to Ali Aladdin at-Tabrizi, "You have no rival in the kingdom of chess, as I have none in government; there is no one to be found that can perform such wonders as I and you, each in his own sphere."

The main religion in Mongolia is Islam, but there seems to be little adherence to the Koran's edict on graven images since all their chess sets are carved figures, conforming to the Buddhist custom, but carved in a distinctive style of their own, in accordance with Mongolian traditions.

An American naval officer serving in Inner Mongolia at the end of World War II was agreeably surprised, when visiting a lama temple, to discover that the monks played chess. When he asked to see one of their sets, a young lama produced a red, lacquered box and a large, wooden, uncheckered board. The chess pieces were carved from willow

LEFT AND RIGHT
The Mongolians have a tradition of carving their sets based on the culture of their local society. As each set is individually carved, rarely are two sets exactly the same. The names of the chessmen also alter to some extent, depending on the district the set originates from. In the set illustrated, the queen is a tiger and the king a local leader, camels are always the two-humped bactrians, the horses are normally, like the camels, without riders, and the rook is usually a cart or the symbol of movement, such as a wheel. The pawns in this set

display the various trades and activities common to Mongolian culture, but they can be any item natural to their society, including domestic and grassland animals.

BELOW *Carved from soapstone, the set represents the Soyot tradition with a king shown as a "noyion" or master of the house in the costume of a wealthy Utyankh. The queen is shown as a sacred lion of Chinese legend, the camel and horse are constant features of a Mongolian set, the rook is shown as a symbol of movement, the pawns are smaller carvings of the sacred lion. Circa 1960. King 2 inches.*

wood, painted and varnished. One side was predominantly red, the other green. The king on the red side was carved as a Mongol prince, opposed by a Chinese viceroy. Next to the king were mythical lions; then, continuing on either side were camels, horses, and carts.

In place of queens were sacred lions from Tibetan-Chinese legends, representing good against evil. The major chess pieces represent important aspects of the normal living requirements of a nomadic existence. The Bactrian camels (bishops) have two humps are native to Mongolia, and capable of traveling long distances without much sustenance. Horses (knights) are the fast-moving ponies that once played a major part in the creation of a great empire, and are still an essential requirement for Mongolian men. Mongol carts (rooks) are small and compact, perfect for nomadic travel, carrying the household belongings and folded animal skins for erecting as their homes. Domestic animals, such as rabbits, hens, goats, and dogs, would be used to depict the pawns. In different parts of Mongolia where customs varied, this difference would be incorporated into the shape of the chess pieces. In Tuva, in northwest Mongolia, the cart is replaced by a huge wheel and the pawns are small mythical Chinese lions.

THAILAND AND CAMBODIA

In the twentieth century both Thailand and Cambodia suffered from devastating wars. Thailand was occupied by the Japanese, who used slave labor to build the infamous bridge over the River Kwai, where an estimated 65,000 people died building the bridge and railway line it carried.

Cambodia was drawn into the Vietnam War, and then came under the dictatorship of Pol Pot—causing millions of people to be killed in the cause of a flawed communist doctrine. Both these countries have shared cultures and history going back to before the last millennium.

At Angkor, in northwest Cambodia, can be seen the magnificent ruins of an earlier civilization which flourished in the ninth to fifteenth centuries. Here are the remains of over 600 elaborately carved Hindu temples, some bigger than cathedrals.

Thailand, is the only country in southeast Asia that was never a European colony. Until 1939 it was known as Siam, famed because of the popular story of Anna and the King of Siam, and the successful film and musical *The King and I*. (Incidentally, Thailand is still a kingdom, under King Rama IX, known as Bhumibol Adulyadej until his accession as a boy after the mysterious death of his elder brother in 1946.)

In the past the cultures of these two countries have been strongly influenced by the dominant religions of the Hindus and Buddhists. Both have strong chess traditions, in

BELOW *The set is carved from Indian ivory, one side stained red, although both sides are the same except for the pawns, which are similar to ones made in Canton. While they seem to differ in style from the major pieces, they definitely belong to the set, and are not replacements. The major pieces are well carved by an experienced master carver, but he appears to be working to satisfy European taste with little knowledge of differences in aesthetic culture. The rooks are frontier forts, each with a standard-bearer holding a flag. The knights are particularly beautifully carved.*

which they have for centuries shared one basic design of chess set, made for conventional chess play.

Generally the sets are turned and carved from teak wood, one side being stained

black. This particular set is ivory opposed by horn; the pawns are cowrie shells that have been cut to a flat base, one side being darker than the other. It is difficult to date such a set; it is obviously of some age, but there are no identifying clues, apart from the patina. While cowrie shells are used as pawns, alternatives are also acceptable, such as small wood counters that match the set. The rook, being a boat, is following the custom of other countries such Russia, Bengal, and Java, where rivers and lakes provide the main highway of travel by boat and as a result boats have taken the place of chariots and carts.

Carved sets are less plentiful in these countries than in Burma, probably because of the popularity of the conventional players' set. It is also possible that some of the Burmese carved figural sets have been made in Thailand, but because of the similarity of design have not been identified as such.

However, there may have been a carving center in Saigon (now Ho Chi Minh City) when it was under French rule as a commercial trading colony. The style appears to be similar to that of the Indian carvers of Berhampur, but mixed with that of Chinese carving made for the European trade.

INDONESIA AND THE PHILIPPINES

Indonesia is a mountainous and heavily forested country consisting of over 13,500 islands separated by miles of sea. The largest of these islands is Java. On the islands, the main religious group follows Islam, but there are also Christians, Hindus, and Buddhists, to provide the usual wide-ranging mix of ethnic cultures found in such diverse countries.

Chess was introduced to these islands from southern India and reinforced by the Arab traders and influenced again by the Portuguese and the Dutch, who from the sixteenth century made Jakarta the center of their trading empire. They ruled Java and most of the islands until 1949.

Chess was popular among the ordinary natives, who would whittle their own sets from soft wood or bamboo, lightly staining one side. There was a regular pattern to the sets they made: the king would be the tallest piece; the queen would be slightly shorter but with a V-cut finish; the bishop would be smaller, topped by a V cut; the knight is again smaller with a diagonal cut; the rook is shaped like the top of a pencil; and the pawns are just small cuts of wood or leaves.

The board, which does not have checkered squares, would simply be scratched into the ground. In Sumatra the game was so popular that it was normal for the village meeting halls to have a chessboard carved into the wood floor.

They were also better-made sets turned in an abstract Muslim pattern, similar to the Indian sets.

BELOW *These are classic Javanese chessmen, in particular the rook, a simple rowing boat. The ratu (king) is seen seated on a throne on an elephant with a mahout; the* pateh *(queen) rides a horse carrying a sword: the* mantri *(bishop) is an elephant controlled by a mahout; the* jaran *(knight) is a horse with rider holding a sword. The* bidaq *(pawns) are soldiers in uniforms and these uniforms provide the best indication to the age of the set. The soldiers are wearing European uniforms and carrying rifles that were still being used in the twentieth century. Because of the rifles, the earliest*

date that can be
considered for the set
would be the end of
the nineteenth
century.

ABOVE *Simply
carved, yet almost
recognizable, bamboo
pieces from Java.*

Surprisingly, despite the enthusiasm of the Javanese for chess
and a reputation on some of the islands for carving, very few
carved ivory sets with carved figures were made. A set that may
have been commissioned from a Javanese carver is illustrated. It
conforms to the nomenclature of Javanese chessmen, the king or
raja is a *ratu*, the queen or minister is a *pateh*, the bishop or
elephant is a *mantri*, the knight or Horse is a *jaran*, the rook or
boat is a *prahn*, the pawn or soldier a *bidaq*.

The Philippines is similar to Indonesia in that it is made up of many islands, in this case more than 7,000. It is in an earthquake zone and is subject to volcanic eruptions and typhoons. The country derived its name from King Philip II of Spain—the islands were under Spanish rule for three centuries. The predominant religions are Roman Catholicism and Islam.

It seems that chess has been popular in the Philippines since it was introduced by the Arab traders who arrived with their traveller's tales and self-imposed standing as prophets of Mohammed, probably around the fourteenth century. In relatively recent times, chess was actively promoted by the late President Ferdinand Marcos. He regarded himself as a personal friend of the chess world champion Bobby Fischer, and tried to persuade him to defend his title against the young Russian challenger Anatoly Karpov, by offering a huge prize fund for the event.

Marcos, infamous for his extravagance in buying *objets d'art*, had an impressive collection of chess sets. In 1978 the world chess championship was held at Baguio City, between the world champion Anatoly Karpov and his challenger Victor Korchnoi. Karpov narrowly won the match, six games to five, with 21 draws. The start of the match was almost delayed when the players discovered that the Filipino organizers expected them to play with

BELOW *A typical conventional set turned from horn, the contrasting colors of white and black obtained by using horn from different animals. The design of the set is very basic, except for the knights, which provide a striking contrast by being so bizarre. The knights' shape has evolved from a horse's head with a flowing mane, and is influenced by the Filipinos' constant fear of tropical storms, erupting volcanoes and earthquakes. To avoid these disasters they have carved into the corners of their roofs a mythical serpent, a*

symbol of good fortune to protect the home from fire and flood. It is this symbol of good fortune that has replaced the horse in a Filipino chess set. Circa 1850. King 2 inches.

a local chess set of a differing design from the usual Staunton set. Such problems did this cause that a messenger was despatched to Manila to find a Staunton set before the match could begin.

When the Arabs first introduced chess to southeast Asia, the sets they played with were not unlike the Islamic ones used in Arabia and Europe during the tenth century. Over the course of time the shape of the pieces changed. Each country or tribal nation developed its own design of conventional playing set. The final pattern of these sets was influenced by the culture of their society. Once established, as in Muslim India, Thailand, and Cambodia, on Java and in the Philippines, they remained, little changed for centuries. Even in this new millennium ancient conventions and their naturally designed chess sets persist.

CHINA

RIGHT *A painting by the English artist, Frampton, of the lovers Miranda and Ferdinand in Shakespeare's play* The Tempest, *in a scene where they play a game of chess as they court one another (a Chinese ivory chess set is depicted on the board.)*

China is the world's most populous country with more than 1,300 million inhabitants and it is one of the world's oldest civilizations. Among the many inventions that came out of ancient China are paper, porcelain, gunpowder, and printing. The Chinese have a long history that includes being the original source of ancient games, such as go and mahjong.

There is a Chinese version of chess, *Xiang Q'I*. It is played on a board of nine by ten lines. The pieces do not move within the squares but on the points or intersections of the lines. There are similarities that suggest that the games chess and *Xiang Q'i* did, at some time in their early history, cross-pollinate, as both games have, or have had, generals, (knight) mandarins (queen) elephants (bishop) horses (knight) chariots (rook) soldiers (pawn). The aim of *Xiang Q'i* is to checkmate the opposing general.

The Chinese believe that Indian chess is a variation of *Xiang Q'i*, while the Indians are confidant that the reverse is the case. Despite the evidence for both, we still don't know the truth, and wait patiently for some definitive evidence.

The pieces for the Chinese game are in the shape of simple discs, as used in checkers, but with the name of each piece inscribed on either side, usually colored red opposed to blue.

There is a Chinese legend that tells how the Emperor Wen Ti came across a group of travelers playing a new game, chess. He noticed they were using carved figures of a rajah, or emperor. He was outraged that anyone would use an effigy of such an exalted personage as an emperor in a mere game. He ordered the immediate execution of the players—as so often happened—and decreed that henceforth no game should be played with images carved in recognizable forms. This has been sited as the reason for the simple form of the game's pieces.

Europeans introduced their form of chess to China in the late eighteenth century, and even then it was due to commerce. The British East India Company, Dutch East India Company, and other trading groups from France, Portugal,

Parliament and the U.S. House of Representatives in 1897. The match was drawn. The set was displayed in the chess room of the House of Commons, where it was placed in two glass cases, the white chessmen in one and the red in the other. That was until 1995, when, during a parliamentary recess, a thief broke one of the cases and stole the red Chinese chessmen.

RIGHT *The Chess Player. An oil painting by Herbert A. Bird, 1929. The set displayed in the painting is an ivory Anglo-Chinese set, carved in Canton to an English design for export to Europe and America.*

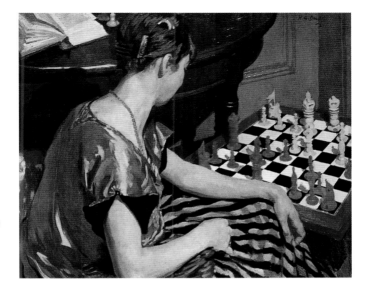

and the newly formed United States of America, all came and established trading posts at the ports of Macau, Hong Kong, Canton, and Shanghai.

There was a great demand in Europe and the U.S.A. for anything Oriental, particularly porcelain, ivory carvings, and objects of virtu. In Canton carving workshops were established for making traditional ivory articles and ivory chess sets for export. There is a strong English influence to the design of the Chinese ivory sets. Possibly, as in Vizagapatam, the sets had originally been commissioned by officials of the British East

India Company. Although all the sets are carved in a very distinctive Chinese fashion, in 90 percent of all the figural sets the king of the white side is George III of England, which would indicate a date sometime in the late eighteenth century when the Chinese began to create these sets. Having established the style for their sets, the carvers continued to use George III as their chess king throughout the following century.

While the carving style of the sets is Chinese by tradition, depicting Chinese figures, the classification of the design is English, with a king, queen, bishop, and knight, and a rook carved as an elephant and castle. The Chinese king is normally described as an emperor or mandarin, but, possibly because the Chinese carvers knew the legend of Emperor Wen Ti and were anxious that they should not

LEFT *A red Emperor Napoleon king.*

BELOW *There were a number of differing designs produced by the carvers of Canton. A particularly attractive design includes decorative stands, turned with surface floral design carving, mounted by figural carved heads threaded to the bases. Most of these sets have the Chinese side dyed red, but occasionally a green dye would be used, as seen here. The English ivory side is left natural. Alex Hammond, in his 1950 book on chessmen, described a similar set thus: "Portuguese, these traditional pieces*

come from Macao in China and have been made in thousands for the Portuguese settlers on that peninsula." Now it is accepted that in a number of cases his attributions were based on speculative assumptions. His stories were, however, so convincing that it has been difficult to convince his loyal clientele that such a set is unlikely to be from Portugal or Macao. A few of these sets have a Chinese cannon as rook, and some have the Duke of Wellington as king. They were probably made to celebrate his victory over Napoleon at Waterloo in 1815.

carve an effigy of their emperor, the Chinese kings and queens are based on costumes used by actors in traditional plays on Chinese mythology.

A favorite for the king in chess is Torgchou, the god of war. He is identified by a ferocious face carved on the front of the costume worn by the king. Occasionally, George III would be replaced by another monarch. On some sets, Emperor Napoleon is portrayed as the king, standing proudly on his plinth, in a familiar stance with his arm crossed over his chest.

Napoleon was a keen chess player, he had been a regular at the Café de la Régence in Paris. When exiled to St. Helena, he spent a lot of time playing the game with his captors. One of his regular opponents was a Lady Malcolm. In "The St. Helena Story" the following chess tale is recalled.

Napoleon sent especially for her [a young girl called Betsy] to come and see "some pretty toys." When she arrived at the billiards room, a cheerful Emperor met her with his usual ear-pinching and enveloping embrace. On the table was a set of chessmen. He had laid them out in rows and pored over them with serried delight. With Lady Malcolm, a good player, he had sat down to play after lunch and, he told Betsy, the beauty of the little figures had put him off his game, Lady Malcolm having beaten him. The figures were executed with exquisite skill, the men representing

all the trades of China. Napoleon, examining the lovely figures, told Betsy they were too nice for St. Helena and he would send them to the King of Rome for him to play with.

Another principal chess tale concerning the Emperor Napoleon was written by William Elphinstone (15th Baron) in *The Catalogue* (c. 1870).

*denying that the skill
of the Chinese carver-
artist is impressive,
and, in this disc set,
one can only take a
deep breath and
wonder how it was
possible for anyone to
have had the
technique, patience,
and skill to produce
such delicate work as
the ivory filigree
pattern of these sets,
and make them
commercially viable.
The chess sets, with the
central carved emblems
of the individual
chess pieces, were made
for export to Britain
and the United States.
They were often
integrated with a
chess/backgammon
board, making a
compendium of three
popular games,
backgammon, checkers,
and chess. However, if
they were used in
earnest, the games
would have to be
played very gently,
as the pieces are not
well designed for
thumping down on
boards and yelling
"Check mate"!*

Napoleon having been civil to Captain J.D. Elphinstone 7 Hussars when wounded at Quatre Bras and taken prisoner, the Hon. Mrs. Elphinstone, his mother, wrote to her son John, then chief of the Factories of the East India Company, at Canton to make a point of visiting the Emperor at St. Helena when he returned from China. John was there on Napoleon's Day when it was customary to make small presents to the Emperor. He gave to the Emperor some Chinese silk shawls and learned that the Emperor was anxious for a set of chessmen. Having none on Board, he sent orders to Canton for a set. On their arrival at St. Helena, Sir Hudson Lowe, the Governor of the Island, would not allow them to be delivered, as the Kings were crowned with what he maintained was the semblance of an Imperial Crown. The set was therefore returned to J. F. Elphinstone.

Another set given to Napoleon, had been especially designed for him by his supporters. It was not until 1933 that, at an exhibition held at Austerlitz of Napoleonic artifacts, the discovery was made that within Napoleon's chess set, made from ivory and mother-of-pearl, was a plan to rescue him from St. Helena. Napoleon had never realized the chessmen had held any secret messages, as the officer bringing the set to Napoleon died while at sea and was thus unable to explain the hidden significance.

These distinctive Chinese chess sets were originally made for export but by the end of the nineteenth century they were also being sold to tourists visiting Hong Kong and Shanghai. As their market expanded, so, unfortunately, did the quality of craftsmanship decline. Due to other unfavorable world events— the wars in Europe, the economic depression, and the Japanese invasion of China—the carving of chess sets ceased, as did most trading. In the 1950s, Chinese ivory carvers were again practicing their skills, working from Hong Kong. The rest of China, under

communist rule, discouraged any trading with the Western Alliance. The Hong Kong ivory carvers did not continue in the traditions of their predecessors but initiated a modified style of carving that embraced their ancient culture. The first obvious change is in the staining: the strong red dye has been replaced by a tea brown, and often the ivory has been lightly stained to create an illusion of patina, normally associated with ancient ivory. The sets tend to be a loose representation of past dynasties, with a Chinese emperor as king and his empress as queen. The bishops are philosophers, the knights, warriors on horseback, the rooks pagodas, and the pawns soldiers—or sometimes, in the better sets, the immortals of Chinese mythology. The best work from this new era of Chinese carvers is very acceptable and they satisfy the prevailing needs of the commercial market. Nevertheless, they will never compete with the artistic nostalgia for the distinctive style and integrity of the earlier sets.

BELOW, FROM LEFT TO RIGHT
These five kings were carved in London, Vizagapatam, Jaipur, Vizagapatam, Canton. The English ivory king, circa 1820, provides an interesting example of the effect on chess-set design and how it can change from the original when it is taken from its natural cultural environment and introduced to an entirely different system of society, with differing religions, aesthetic tastes, and skill conventions. Each of the five chess pieces shown is individually well crafted, aesthetically pleasing, practical in design, and completely different—but obviously related.

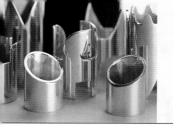

"I played chess with him and would have beaten him sometimes, only he always took back his last move, and ran the game out differently."

—Mark Twain, *Life on the Mississippi*

The twentieth century would see miraculous advances in science and technology, particularly in the fields of medicine, transportation, and communications. No one on January 1, 1900, celebrating the beginning of a new century, could have imagined that, during the next hundred years, man would be able to command instant light at the touch of a switch, could, at a whim, fly to any part of the globe, or sit at home and watch moving pictures in color of men walking on the moon. Nor would they have believed that many incapacitating diseases would be cured, and some eliminated. The achievement of organ transplantation could not remotely have been considered and there would have

ABOVE AND PREVIOUS PAGE *Cy Endfield's silver chessmen designed in 1972 to commemorate the Fischer-Spassky world championship match —a set designed to be practical, easy to handle and stable on the board, contained in a leather case, convenient to pack into a traveling bag.*

LEFT *The first women's International Tournament held in London 1897 was won by Miss Mary Rudge of England. Many ladies represented their countries. Mrs Stephenson came from Canada, Mrs Worrall from the U.S., Mrs Perry from Ireland, Mrs Muller-Hartog from Germany and Mrs Fagan from Italy. The gentlemen were worried that they would not have the stamina to last the two weeks of competition. In the event, only one lady withdrew due to ill health.*

been no understanding of why millions of people, all around the world, would hold a small black box to their ears while apparently talking to themselves. As for computers and the Internet, these would be considered completely out of this world.

Yet, these same people at the end of the nineteenth century, would have been saddened to know that continual political strife would divide nations, causing disastrous wars that, with the advancement in military technology, have brought about the worst destruction by human upon human in the history of mankind.

It seems the legendary monkeys of good, led by Hanuman, with his qualities of great strength and wisdom, are still needed to continue their battle against the evil demons of Ravana the ten-headed demon king.

By 1900, New York had superseded London as the Mecca for chess players. Wilhelm Steinitz (1836–1900) had established a reputation as the world's best player back in the 1870s, when the Hungarian chess master Johann J. Lowenthal wrote, "Mr Steinitz may be fairly regarded as the present occupant of the exceptional position formerly held by Mr Morphy." Steinitz who had settled in New York and became an United States citizen, was recognized as the official World Chess Champion in 1886, when he defeated Zukertort in a match played at three venues: New York, St. Louis, and New Orleans. Steinitz eventually lost the title in 1894 to Emmanual Lasker of Germany. At this time the American and

European art world went through a renaissance. Convention and tradition were being questioned, new ideas being experimented with. The public were being bombarded with one new art movement, only to be quickly bombarded with another. Art Nouveau was succeeded by Art Deco. Among artists working in these styles there would usually be some who would design and produce a chess set in that mode.

In 1924 Josef Hartwig designed a simple wooden set in the Bauhaus style. Man Ray, who was an avid chess player, had a close affinity with both the Dada and Surrealist movements. He designed many original chess sets. The first was in 1920, in the Dada tradition of taking an object and presenting it in a different form. Ray created a chess set from the items found in his artist's studio: some geometric objects, the broken neck of a violin, a vase, and a sphere. With his artist's insight he transformed them into a modern work of twentieth-century art. A pyramid became a king, a cone a queen, a vase a bishop, a broken violin neck a knight, a cube a rook, and a sphere secured to a button for a base became a pawn. This Man Ray chess set, which can be seen at the Museum of Modern Art in New York, has been the inspiration for many of the modern abstract-designed chess sets that have ensued since. Man Ray designed several other chess sets, including one that he thought might replace the Staunton set as the standard set for use in competitive tournaments.

ABOVE *Early twentieth-century German silver and ivory chess set—as stolen by Ryan O'Neal in the film* The Thief that Came to Dinner.

He approached the American chess champion Frank Marshal for his opinion. Marshal, seeing a modern abstract-designed chess set for the first time, asked if it was meant to be played with! Man Ray asked Marshal if he thought it could be used for chess tournaments. Marshal, who could play a number of games simultaneously without sight of the board, replied that as far as he was concerned, the shape of the chess pieces was irrelevant: he could play with buttons, or even without a chess set.

Marcel Duchamp and Man Ray were close friends and chess partners. Duchamp, being a player of master strength, was selected four times to play for France in international events. Man Ray would often repeat the story of an incident that happened to Duchamp while he honeymooned with his first wife.

"Duchamp spent most of the first week they lived together studying chess problems," he said, "and his bride, in desperate retaliation, got up one night when he was asleep and glued the chess pieces to the board. They were divorced three months later."

It may have been this incident that inspired Man Ray's photo of the chess player, concentrating on the game and showing no surprise that his opponent was a beautiful attractive nude woman.

As with Man Ray, Duchamp's interest in chess was to influence his art. In 1910 he had painted *The Chess Game,* a scene

of his two brothers playing chess while their wives relaxed beside them in the family garden. Duchamp painted this scene in his "Impressionist" style. Later he reproduced the scene in his Cubist mode. He also painted in this same style his well-known oil-on-canvas work, *The Chess Players*, which hangs in the National Museum of Art, New York.

Duchamp practiced his art in many of the new movements. He designed and created a Dada pocket chess set of leather with pinheads to secure the celluloid chess pieces, so they could not be moved, thereby converting a chess set into an art object.

Duchamp organized an art exhibition, with works of art being donated by patrons and artists. The list included works by Picasso, Dali, Matisse,

Tanguy, Johns, and himself. After the exhibition the paintings and other exhibits were sold by auction at the Park-Bernet Gallery, New York. The proceeds, providing substantial capital, were donated to the Duchamp Chess Endowment Foundation, a fund providing support to young, talented U.S. chess masters.

In 1944, Man Ray organized an exhibition in New York, *The Imagery of Chess*. The exhibits were abstract chess sets provided and designed by Modernist artists, including Max Ernst, Man Ray himself, Marcel Duchamp, Yves Tanguy, Alexander Calder, and Julian Levy. These sets were all created from the imaginations of the artists. Such a collection had never been seen before. They emphasized the ideals of the modernist movement in art, breaking down the old traditions and making their own statement that art is the product of a free imagination.

Yves Tanguy created a simple design for a set made from a broom handle. Alexander Calder presented a set of wooden bases, with screws and bent metal placed into the wood—a different metal shape to portray each of the six different chess forms. Julian Levy based his design on egg shells. He explains how he saved the empty shells from his soft-boiled eggs and used their shape to cast the chessmen. Max Ernst produced the most striking set, creating a completely new abstract design, unaware that, back in the tenth

ABOVE *Austrian conventional chessmen made from fruit wood, popular in the Vienna chess clubs and cafés during the first part of the twentieth century. The design is similar to the Staunton, and just as practical for the serious players of the game. The knight is attractively carved and the bishop is in the tradition of sets from eastern Europe with its reverse black hat finial.*

RIGHT *A wooden set inspired by Yves Tanguy abstract design of a set made from a broom handle, which he displayed at the New York exhibition,* The Imagery of Chess *in 1944. This set was also simply cut out of a broom handle, the opposing sides painted orange and purple to create a practical abstract designed chess set.*

BOTTOM RIGHT *The* King Playing with the Queen *by Max Ernst. The design of the chessmen used for this bronze, which was cast in 1954, are similar to the chess set exhibited at the 1944 New York exhibition,* The Imagery of Chess. *This set was given as a gift to Marcel Duchamp, who in turn shared it with his second wife, "Teeny".*

century, the Russian citizens of Novrogrod might well, had they seen it, have assumed it was one of theirs. Max Ernst experimented with differing materials and had a number of sets made from his designs.

One such set, at the Philadelphia Museum of Art, was donated by a chess-set collector and architect named John F. Harbeson. He had been responsible for the architectural arrangement of United States Battle Monuments, maintained in the many countries where U.S. servicemen have seen active service. Max Ernst gave the first of his sets as a thank-you gift to his long-term friend Marcel Duchamp.

A second attempt at marriage by Duchamp was much more successful, probably because "Teeny," his wife—having allowed him to teach her how to play chess—made a pact that they were never to play each other.

In January 1991, the Tate Gallery in London held an exhibition, *Art and Chess.* Teeny Duchamp attended the opening as the guest of honor; it happened to be her 80th birthday. Among the events were a number of chess-related art films, including one

directed by Hans Richer. The film had a sequence showing Max Ernst in his studio working on his chess set. Madame Duchamp was surprised, as she had always regarded the Max Ernst set as hers, given to her by her husband, who she assumed had made it. She was heard to exclaim, referring to the film sequence, "I didn't know he [Ernst] had made it."

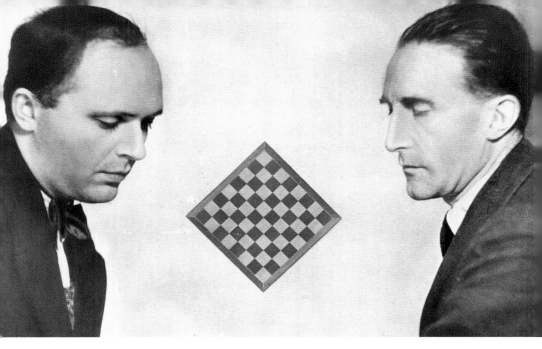

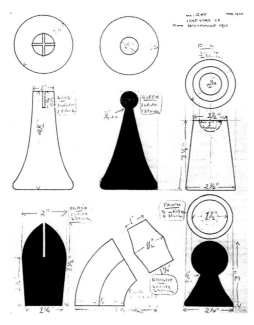

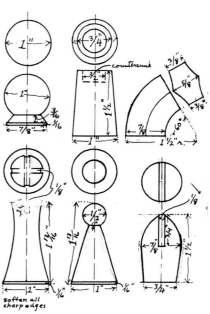

LEFT *Photo taken by Man Ray of his friend Duchamp, seen on the right, and French chess master Vitaly Halberstadt. They both played for the French team in the 1928 chess Olympiads, led by world champion Alexander Alekhine.*

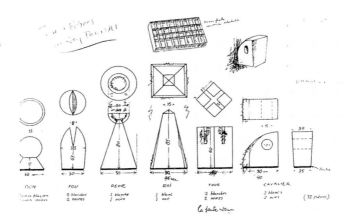

ALL OTHER PICTURES *Man Ray's personal designs for modern abstract chessmen. Some of these were done between 1943 and 1946. The designs were manufactured in limited editions. One set made in silver and red anodized aluminum was contained in a cigar box. Another chess set, a variation on the central design shown here, was made from polished bronze, and came with a wooden table and an inlaid metal chessboard. Man Ray produced it in a limited edition of 50, with one king signed by him.*

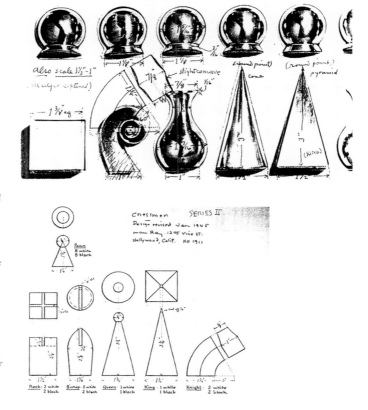

WAR AND CHESS

The normal commercial and social society of the twentieth century was interrupted for a second time in the 1940s for another insane global war involving the United States, Europe, and the Far East. Normal commercial trade, manufacturing, and matters of artistic culture were sacrificed as everything and everyone concentrated solely on the war effort. It meant that much entertainment and many cultural events had to be initiated by individual enterprise.

Large armies do not live by bread alone: they have to have some form of entertainment in order to counteract boredom and maintain good spirits. Providing such facilities is of great important so as to prevent the monotony of waiting when not directly involved in battle.

Games play a primary role in maintaining good moral, and at most army camps accommodation was specifically provided for this purpose: a barrack room, where servicemen could relax and play cards, pool, table tennis, checkers, or chess.

John Jaques & Son, sports manufactures and makers of the Staunton chess sets, were among the early casualties of the war, their premises in central London being directly hit in 1940 by a

LEFT *President Josip Broz Tito of Yugoslavia was a serious chess player. When the Chess Olympiad was held at Dubrovnik he was a regular attendant and mixed freely with the grandmasters. Because his interest in chess was well known, he inadvertently obtained a collection of chess sets as diplomatic gifts from many of the ambassadors posted to Belgrade. He appears to be playing a game with one of these gifts, but seems to be cheerfully undecided as to his next move.*

cluster of incendiary bombs. The premises were burned out, and the only surviving record was a pattern book, which included the designs of the chess sets they made. The book had been kept in a safe but the heat of the fire had been so great it caused the drawings to be singed around the edges. Jaques & Son soon found new premises in a London suburb, where they received orders from the war office to provide large quantities of chess sets for the armed forces. They had no basic materials, because hardwoods had been commandeered for priority war projects. Jaques resolved the problem by obtaining an engineering machine able to press softwood into the shape of a chess piece. They left the pressed chessmen unpolished and unvarnished, staining only one side black. For boxes, Jaques used their reserve prewar stock to hold the chessmen. Probably this is the only time when the boxes were of a better quality than the chess sets they held.

Jaques, like many other manufacturers and exporters, were approached by the British secret service for their views on how information could be concealed within a Red Cross parcel, so that confidential information could be sent to Allied prisoners. The prisoners knew that, if they received a parcel from an unknown relative, that parcel was to be thoroughly searched.

German soldiers, too, were supplied with chess sets, which were provided in a cardboard games package, containing a board for chess and merles, and a chess set in the shape of flat paper discs. The cardboard container had been specifically designed in

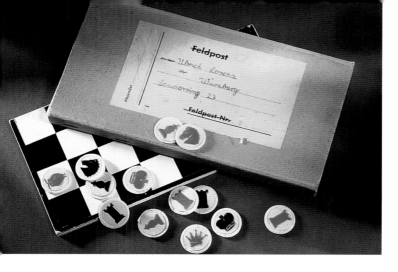

the form of an envelope, with space for a soldier's name, address, and field post number. It had also been designed to be a convenient size for carrying in an army backpack.

In some British factories, despite the fact that they were working around the clock for the war effort, workers could still find time to "borrow" the machine tools and use them to make personal items for their private utilization.

The factory management would normally tolerate this unauthorized activity, and, at certain times, even encourage it.

ABOVE *A chess set
made from cartridges
during World War II.
The ingenuity of the
chess-set makers at
this time was
astounding. The
pieces resemble classic
set design, in
particular the stylized
horse's head that
represents the knight.*

At Christmas many of the factories would allow their engineering
equipment to be unofficially used to make presents and children's
toys. These would then be raffled within the factory and the funds
forwarded to the Red Cross.

A few chess sets were created in this manner. One that has
endured was made at a munitions factory. The set is made out of
empty copper ammunition cartridges, in an imaginative peg
design. An oak board was fitted with painted maroon squares,
each square having a central hole, which had been perfectly placed
by an engineering machine drill.

Individuals were also discovering imaginative ways to combat
the shortages of war. Like the Dada artists, but for a different
purpose, imagination was focused on materials and articles that
could be recycled and used for another new purpose. Women's
organizations meeting in village halls arranged knitting and
quilting parties using material from old clothing.

At the London suburb of Carshalton, a branch of the Women's
Volunteer Service found a use for old cotton reels. They designed
and made a chess set. The cotton reels were used for the bases of
the pieces, and the set was completed with plywood, cut out in a
silhouette fretwork pattern of chessmen, copying the outline of an
old English chess set. The set came in a bag made out of black-out
material. This material was the closely woven black cloth used to
curtain windows during the war—it made certain that no shaft of

light could escape from a building to be seen from above by enemy aircraft. It was extremely important that no one accidentally help the navigators on enemy planes to identify an area for bombing.

Another group who had to solve the dilemma of boredom and lack of facilities were prisoners of war. Some camps organized chess clubs. The chessboards were made out of scraps of paper or simply scratched onto tables or floors. Chessmen would be whittled from broken pieces of wood or molded from stale bread.

Some of the prisoners of war in Hong Kong managed to pack sets in their kitbags, but there were not enough sets to run a club. The balance had to be produced in the camp itself. The skilled soldiers of the British Army Royal Ordnance Corps were just the men for the job. They had been allowed, or had managed, to retain some of the tools of their trade, and were soon able to furnish the Shomshuipo (Deep Water Shore) Chess Club with enough chess sets to make the club viable and to organize a camp tournament. The sets had been carved from oak doors that had been severely bomb-damaged during the battle for Hong Kong. The boards were drawn on any available old or used piece of paper or cardboard.

The Shomshuipo Chess Club Championship ended on July 23, 1942. This did not bring chess to an immediate end in the camp, but malnutrition was taking its toll and no more tournaments were held that year.

In Britain, Italian and German war prisoners were kept in prison camps, but, apart from the German SS officers, they were allowed, under supervision, to volunteer for work during the summer harvesting on local farms, which were starved of manpower. Many friendships were made between soldiers and people in the local community. Some prisoners of war decided to stay on after the hostilities, and settle, marring local women.

As prisoners, they too, had to use their initiative to amuse themselves during the quiet periods spent in prison camps, and

ABOVE A set made by the Carshalton Women's Volunteer Service from cotton reels. Note the blackout curtain bag. The set has been well made by a handy person who knew how to use a fret saw and to secure the cut out chess figures to the cotton reel bases. The set was finished by being painted brown and red, then given a coat of varnish. It's been made so well that the chessmen have, so far, survived over sixty years.

ABOVE *One of the chess sets made from damaged oak doors for the Hong Kong, Shomshuipo prison chess club, by soldiers of the British Ordnance Corps, enabling the club to hold a camp chess tournament in 1942.*

also made their own chess sets. These were particularly popular among the German prisoners. Whittled chess sets made by them, crudely carved but made in a pattern, used designs that were popular in northern Europe throughout the nineteenth century and into the twentieth. The carver would have made the set to a familiar design, probably remembering a family chess set that may have been his father's when he was a child.

RIGHT *Chessmen made by a German war prisoner, stationed in England. The set, whittled from wood, resembles the design of a chess set popular in northern Europe since the nineteenth century. It's not known for certain if this set was made during World War I or II.*

IMAGINATION RULES, OK?

After the war it took a few decades, and aid under the Marshall Plan, for European society to recover from the economic catastrophe that had occurred. The communist government of the Soviet Union, as part of a propaganda policy, encouraged and promoted the game of chess as an example of the benefits of communist ideology. Chess grandmasters were allowed special privileges that were not available to the ordinary Soviet citizen.

Alexander Alekhine was the first Russian to become a world chess champion. He defeated the Cuban Jose Raul Capablanca at Buenos Aires in 1927. Although Alekhine had been a member of the Communist Party, he did not return to Russia after his victory. Instead he decided to reside in France.

In 1946, soon after the war, negotiations were in progress to arrange a world championship match between Alekhine and the Russian grandmaster Mikhail Botvinnik, when Alekhine died suddenly of a heart attack. The World Chess Federation organized a tournament between the world's best chess players to decide who would be the new world champion. A tournament was organized in 1948. It was agreed that it be played at two venues: the first half was held at the Hague in Holland, the second in Moscow. Mikhail Botvinnik took first position and became the new world champion.

Botvinnik was the ideal champion for the communist U.S.S.R —he believed in their ideals, remained a genuine amateur, obtained a doctorate in science, and achieved international eminence as an electrical engineer. The Soviets dominated world

BELOW *A set in silver designed by Cy Endfield to commemorate the 1972 world chess championship match between America's Bobby Fischer and Boris Spassky, the Russian world champion. It is a good example of an abstract design where the individual pieces are easily recognized and are practical enough to play a serious game of chess.*

chess for the next 35 years. During this period Botvinnik lost his title to Vasily Smyslov, regained it, lost it to the brilliant Mikhail Tal, and regained it again. Eventually, Botvinnik lost the title to the Armenian Tigran Petrosian, and retired from competitive chess.

Petrosian defended the world championship twice. On both occasions his opponent was Boris Spassky. Petrosian won the first match to retain the title. The second match, in 1969, was won by Spassky, who become the world champion. In 1972 the Soviet dominance of the world chess championship was challenged by a unique personality, matured within the capitalist culture of America: Robert James (Bobby) Fischer, brought up in Brooklyn, New York. Bobby, from age six, was completely absorbed by chess. Aged 14, he became the United States' chess champion.

Spassky versus Fischer: the match of the century

The Spassky–Fischer world championship match in Reykjavík, Iceland, was proclaimed by the international press as the "match of the century." It was to be more dramatic off the board than on it. Never has a chess match had so much media coverage. They pronounced the contest as a war of ideologies, capitalism against communism.

Fisher, having achieved his ambition to challenge the world chess champion, was in emotional turmoil, making all kinds of unreasonable demands of the Icelandic organizers, even risking his own good

BELOW *Icelandic cartoonist H. Petursson captures the essence of the 1972 world championship match by portraying the different cultures that influenced the background to this contest, when he portrays Spassky as a dancing Cossack, representing the U.S.S.R., and Bobby Fischer as a cowboy from the U.S.A., too quick on the draw.*

chances of winning by not arriving for the official opening ceremony. He did eventually arrive—but only after a pleading letter from the American Secretary of State, Henry Kissinger, and an extra £50,000 added to the prize fund by the British financier Jim Slater.

ABOVE *The complete Cy Endfield set, showing the interlocking silver and silver gilt chess pieces alongside the folded board (made of silver and leather), presented within a leather wallet.*

Spassky won the first game. Fischer complained about the film cameras and ordered their removal. He refused to play the second game as the cameras were still in place. The game was recorded as a win to Spassky by default. Two–nil. It appeared that the match would be canceled. Convinced that there would be no further games, many reporters and spectators left Iceland. However, Spassky, determined that the match should continue, agreed to Fisher's irrational request that they should play the third game in a private room, without spectators or cameras. Fischer played brilliantly, winning his first ever game against Spassky. The players moved back to the hall for the remainder of the match, but without the cameras. Fischer went on to win by four clear games.

Having broken the Soviet domination, Fischer withdrew from competitive chess for 20 years. In 1992 he again played Spassky, claiming it was a world championship match. This time the prize fund was $5,000,000, sponsored by a Yugoslavian financier. The match was played in Serbia. Fischer won again, maintaining his own world title. He has not played since, nor has he returned to the United States, as he is likely to be arrested for ignoring the U.S. government sanctions in place on Serbia at time.

To commemorate the first Fischer–Spassky match, a silver chess set was designed and manufactured in a limited edition by Cy Endfield, film director, author, magician, and silversmith. Cy Endfield (1914–95) was best known as the director of *Zulu*, the film that gave the British actor Michael Caine his first starring role. Endfield wrote the book *Zulu Dawn*, a history of the Zulu people, which emerged from the close working relationship he cultivated with Zulus while filming at Rourk's Drift.

Endfield was also an accomplished magician. *The Times* of London put him in a list of the world's top ten. Endfield was also a qualified silversmith, entitled to use his own silver hallmark of "c e" within an escutcheon shield. Born in the United States, he moved to England in 1950 in protest over the McCarthy investigation of communism within Hollywood.

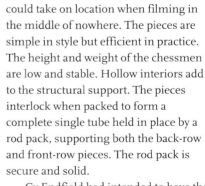

Cy Endfield's Fischer–Spassky portable set is a masterpiece of practical abstract design, yet based on the same feudal symbolism as those of the Staunton sets. The castle's tower, the horse's head of the knight, the mitered bishop, and the crown and coronet of the king and queen are in a style clearly influenced by the architectural tenets of the twentieth-century abstract movements. This is not surprising, given that one of Endfield's closest chess-playing friends since their student days when they shared lodgings, was the artist and photographer Man Ray.

The set was designed to be light to carry, with a board that opens to a practical size for a game. Endfield wanted a set that was attractive and lightweight, durable and compact—one that he

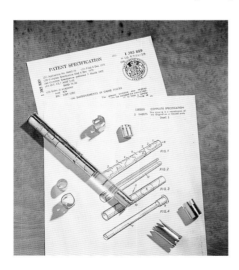

could take on location when filming in the middle of nowhere. The pieces are simple in style but efficient in practice. The height and weight of the chessmen are low and stable. Hollow interiors add to the structural support. The pieces interlock when packed to form a complete single tube held in place by a rod pack, supporting both the back-row and front-row pieces. The rod pack is secure and solid.

Cy Endfield had intended to have the first 100 sets engraved with Fischer's and Spassky's signatures on the king of each set. Spassky signed but Fischer refused: he felt it was against his

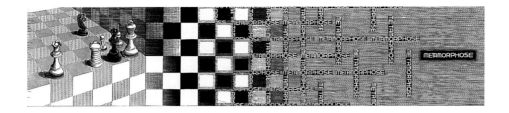

principles. A limited number of sets were offered for sale by the London *Sunday Times*; they were all immediately sold, the offer being greatly oversubscribed.

Modernism and the abstract

Abstract art had been considered avant garde during the first part of the century. Owing to the promotion of experimental modes of art and design by the Modernist movement, abstract art has become accepted as a respectable form of artistic expression with its own genre. As Man Ray and Duchamp were among the first to realize, the scope and variety of design in the creation of abstract decorative chess sets is infinite. These sets also had the advantage that they could be produced in limited numbers to coincide with fashion trends, or created to meet the tastes of particular interests.

Sets of the same genre as Cy Endfield's have been produced by many artists. It is often apparent from the design whether the artist is a chess player—because he would know just how to mix a decorative element with the practical requirements of a set—or whether he has little knowledge of the game and produces, as I have seen, 32 pieces that refuse to harmonize or even stand together. However, the majority of these sets are well thought out, are attractive, and can be played with. An example of such a set can be seen in the American television situation comedy *Frasier*, where the chess set's prime purpose is to be an aesthetic object that adds to and harmonizes with the decor of a modern avant-garde intellectual apartment. (In episodes of *Frasier*, the set can be seen standing on the table in front of the mock fireplace.)

An interesting example is provided by a minimalist chess set, designed by David Pelham and produced in London in 1970. It is a complete concept to attune the board, the set, the pieces, and the

ABOVE *On Escher's metamorphic chess board the game continues and changes, and continues and changes, and continues to change until the game is metamorphosed again. Then it changes again ...*

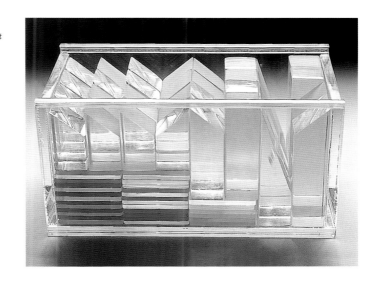

material. It is made from acrylic, and contrast is achieved by having transparent and opaque pieces. The box is made from transparent acrylic, precisely measured so as to contain the board, which consists of 64 individual squares, half of them transparent and the other half opaque. The pieces are designed to be placed in a predetermined pattern in order to allow the box to be closed. The chessmen are of a very simple design, all of the same cubiform dimensions, but varying in height. Some pieces—the queen, knight, and pawn—have a right-angle diagonal cut at their topmost point, while the bishops have a more acute angled diagonal cut. When these chessmen are set in a straight line, the

pieces next to each other, they can easily be mistaken for an outline of an architect's model for a modern skyscraper city, similar to the silhouetted views seen from offshore New York and Chicago.

Sets of abstract design have been an irresistible challenge to many modern artists, who have created imaginative specimens out of differing substances, such popular themes being nuts and bolts, bent nails, designer paper, marbles of differing size and color, Pepsi and Coca-Cola cans, sea shells, perfume bottles, 80,000,000-year-old ammonite fossils, bulls' teeth, crystal glass, bog wood, car engine components, and even marzipan.

A set created by the London artist Barry Martin and exhibited at the Tate Gallery was made out of King Edward potatoes; he chose this particular brand of potato because they would be portraying the "Royal Game."

Creations in ceramics

Modern technology in pottery has enabled individual ceramic artists to work within their studios with their personal kiln, allowing them to fire and complete their own ceramic creations. Many potters now work in small groups, able to form modest ceramic workshops. Local potters living in tourist towns produce ceramic artifacts as quality souvenirs for town visitors. Attractive chess sets are often included as a part of their stock. A pottery in the picturesque town of Rye on England's south coast produced a very striking set, with kings nine inches in height. The set is

BELOW *R.C. Kew's ceramic masterpiece inspired by Martin Bros. chess set from the turn of the twentieth century. From the left, a "good" Arthurian king, with his queen and praying bishop protected by the white knight next to a fortified castle tower, with a pawn made in the image of Wallace Martin, founder of Martin Bros. Potters, 1876. The evil side of the set starts with a pawn grimacing up at the dark fortifications on a hill, protected by a monster knight and a menacing Merlin standing next to a miserable queen seated by the side of a demon king uncomfortably seated on his throne contemplating his next dastardly deed.*

brightly colored in glazed crimson versus a strong purple. It is based on the town's early history, when Vikings frequently raided English coastal fortified ports. The chessmen are presented in a modern stylized form. The only difference between the feuding

ABOVE AND RIGHT
Chessmen made by
the Martin Bros. Top,
from the left: knight,
knight, king, pawn,
queen, pawn rook,
bishop, rook.
Center, two knights
and two pawns.

sides is the rooks. On one side they are hill forts, and are opposed by one-mast galleons—now the ship emblem of the town in the shape of a model similar to the fifteenth-century vessels used by Columbus when he set sail to America.

Some individual potter artists are inspired by ceramic concepts and styles from the past. That was the situation for R.C. Kew. He admired the artistic products of the Martin Brothers, who in 1876 established a pottery in Southall, a district of London. Dr. Gray of Harvard University was a frequent visitor to the Martin Brothers'

showrooms in London. An admirer and collector of their wares, he obtained inscribed Martin Ware cups for the winning eight in the Harvard–Yale boat race. The Martin Brothers also made a punch bowl for the Bohemian Club of San Francisco. It was designed as a large owl, but it was destroyed in the earthquake of 1906.

The eldest brother, Robert Wallace Martin, was the one whose creative ability and imagination made him a leading force in the English potters' expansion during the late nineteenth century. Martin Ware is remembered today for grotesque birds, character pots, and jugs, which have become so desired by collector connoisseurs that they obtain amazingly high prices at auction. However Martin Brothers also produced a wide range of objects, designing

and manufacturing a great deal of architectural ornamentation for building façades, many of which still exist.

Wallace Martin designed two complete chess sets. His first was made for a collector, Victor Hodgson, a stockbroker. This set later passed to one Ernest Marsh. The second set designed and made by the Martin Brothers was smaller than the first, but the bishops, which are the tallest pieces in the set, measured 5 inches. Made in 1902, it was sold to a Mrs. Boulnois for £25. Now it can be seen displayed at the Victoria and Albert Museum, London.

Wallace's younger brothers tried to discourage him from making these chess sets, because they took an excessive amount of time, which could have been used to produce more commercially viable products. This may be the reason why no further sets were made, but Wallace did create duplicate pieces. There are seven of his chessmen at the City of Plymouth Museum: a king, a bishop, two pawns, and three rooks.

R.C. Kew, having seen the Martin Brothers' chess set at the museum, was inspired by the character of the set to try to complement the work of Wallace Martin, by striving to recapture the style and the vivacity projected by the individual pieces. Kew has followed and incorporated many of the Wallace ideas for individual chessmen: the bishops are similar in design; the kings and queens are shown sitting on thrones in a like manner, but are more extreme in style. Kew also presents a clear theme of the white side representing good, in an Arthurian Camelot environment, against a mythological underworld ruled by a

ABOVE AND LEFT *A white-side Martin Bros. bishop with his crozier, a symbol of the bishop's authority. Left. The king and queen from the dark side of the Martin Bros. set. The Martin ware chess men are on permanent display in the ceramic gallery of the Victoria and Albert Museum. The style of the brothers ceramic objects, including their chessmen, were generations in advance of their time. It is only since the last part of the 20th century, with the advance in ceramic technology has it been possible for other potters to match the imaginative creations of the Martin Bros.*

demon king, with Merlin bishops and monster knights to face the imperishable white knights of Round Table legends. Wallace spiced his sets with cameo humor, such as the castle guard with his trousers down, and the eight individual pawns as jesters.

Kew, likewise, introduces humor into the set with his pawns. On the dark side he has them competing in a gurning (or face-pulling) festival, to see who can make the most grotesque face, while on the good side he has portrait busts of the five Martin brothers: Wallace is an old gray bearded man wearing spectacles; Walter has a handsome black beard; Charles has an admirable handlebar mustache; Edwin and James both have thick, black, bushy mustaches and are difficult to differentiate, except for Edwin's bushy eyebrows. Kew is obviously an accomplished ceramic artist, and he certainly produced a set that Wallace Martin would have appreciated.

In loving memory: the souvenir industry

The souvenir industry is an essential part of the tourist trade. It produces and decides which artifacts are likely to be of greatest interest for its visitors. The result is that tourist destinations throughout the globe have created souvenirs to mirror aspects of their local culture and history.

The carvers of Bali in Indonesia are well organized to supply all kinds of imaginative items, from exotic furniture to miniature frogs carved from local teak—and made to a professional and often impressive standard. They, too, provide chess sets that are designed to represent their ancient culture, and yet meet the modern preferences of their tourist guests. A chess set of frogs playing musical instruments is one of their interesting themes.

African tribes also have carvers who have adapted to the commercial advantages of exporting their wares, carving in the style of their ancestors for the pleasure of their new customers. Such sets are imported to Europe and the United States from Nigeria, Sierra Leone, Senegal, Mali, Ghana, Congo, and Zimbabwe. Most are naïvely but charmingly carved from local woods—ivory and soapstone—while a few are made from metal and painted. Most of the sets are a representation of their own tribal ethnic culture.

Europe also has a number of outlets that manufacture figural decorative sets, mainly molded from metals, plastics, and resins. In Melegnano, a small town south of Milan, Italy, Piero Benzonia, a silversmith who also works in pewter and bronze, designs and creates his own artifacts under the name of "Bronzi d'Arte." He produces a range of art chess sets. Very attractively made from metals trimmed with gilding, they have a number of medieval themes and bear titles—such as the "Medieval" set, which has the chessmen wearing clothing inspired by costumes worn in fifteenth-century England. An unusual theme is one made with animals produced as silver versus gold: the king and queen are a lion and lioness, a bear acts as bishop, a giraffe replaces the knight, the rook is a sitting elephant, and the pawns are monkeys. Italy has a number of firms manufacturing

BELOW *A delightful African set carved in Nigeria from light and dark thorn-wood. The figures represent the Yoruda from southwestern Nigeria. The rooks are thatched huts, the knight is a rider on a small pony, the*

bishop holds a cross, and the king and queen are a tribal chief and his wife. They are all dressed in local fashion. The pawns, each one with a different expression, could represent the undernourished children of Africa.

decorative chess sets, which are available from the stores of large towns and tourist resorts.

An English manufacturer makes good figural sets from a resin compound molded into sets that depict popular national themes, such as Sherlock Holmes, *Alice's Adventures in Wonderland*, and Robin Hood. Some are finished by hand painting but the majority are brown on one side against cream.

One of the most popular tourist attractions in Britain's capital city is the Tower of London, where Anne Boleyn, the second wife of Henry VIII, had her head chopped off in 1536. A set based on Henry VIII with him as king has the tower as a rook, and Cardinal Thomas Wolsey (1475–1530) as the bishop; the queen is probably Henry's sixth wife, Catherine Parr, who survived him by a year, to die in 1548. The set could be made more interesting by having an option of Ann Boleyn as the queen in the form of her ghost, which has been seen haunting the tower, walking with her head tucked underneath her arm.

Greece, has an ancient civilization that can be traced back to before the fifth century B.C., when Athens defeated the all-powerful Persian army at the Battle of Marathon. Athens created the world's first democracy and established a culture that has had a major influence on Western civilization. The Parthenon in Athens and the sculpture *Venus de Milo* are good examples of the extraordinarily advanced standard achieved by the ancient Greeks in art and architecture.

This background—together with permanent blue skies, impressive scenery, and the many historical architectural sites with their ancient temples and coliseums—has made modern Greece a favorite destination for teachers, students, scholars, and sun-seeking tourists alike.

The souvenir industry is possibly too well organized: there is a proliferation of choice, based on the art of Greece's ancient culture, such as statuettes of the *Venus de Milo* and other artifacts offered in their thousands. Included in this extravaganza—with streets of souvenir shops offering the same items—will be a selection of chess sets in nearly every shop, almost all of them featuring Alexander the Great.

The sets made to represent Alexander and his army are all of the same design but vary in size and material: some are molded from plastic, others from metal. The quality is of an acceptable souvenir standard, and they are usually sold with a marble board that harmonizes well with the set. They certainly succeed in being a very acceptable memento of an enjoyable vacation.

Plastics and Tinseltown

American technology in plastics seems to have reached its zenith. There appears to be no challenge that cannot be met. One could say that reproduction of any commodity from a plastic composite, in the brightest of colors, has become child's play.

This is especially true with regard to film characters created for American television cartoon series, and Hollywood fantasy and action blockbuster films.

The Wizard of Oz was one of the first to have a chess set made using characters from the film. The Lion was king, Dorothy the queen, Scarecrow became the bishop, and the Tin Man the knight, while the rook was an enchanted castle. James Bond and the TV series *Star Trek* have also inspired themes for chess sets. *Star Trek* producers created their own form of intergalactic chess, to be played on three levels with the pieces able to move from one level to another—a game to challenge Mr. Spock's intellectual capacity.

At any Disney World theme park it should be possible to obtain a set depicting Snow White complete with the Seven Dwarfs and/or a Mickey Mouse set. Some of the latest chess sets to be found among blockbuster film merchandise are those associated with the 1999 Star Wars "prequel" movie, *The Phantom Menace*, and the popular television series, *The Simpsons*. These sets are made primarily for fun, and playing a game of chess with

such a set stimulates the kidding area of the brain and, over the battleground of the board, you can be as silly or as stupid as Homer Simpson, or as brave or foolhardy as Bart. Because these sets are manufactured in enormous numbers and are available at a modest cost, it is easy to overlook the quality of the product. The accuracy of the detail in the three-dimensional reproduction of the chessmen is very authentic. The finished articles produced for these chess sets and for similarly made toys pays a fitting compliment to the standard achieved by the plastics industry. The problem of quality versus quantity seems, at least in this area of production, to have been resolved, and both objectives are possible.

BELOW *Alexander the Great represents the past glories of Greece in this plastic molded set of white and black. Alexander is king, his wife, queen. One of his*

BELOW *Plasic molded set featuring the characters of the hit cartoon series 'The Simpsons.' This set has the added humor of the king portrayed as Homer Simpson, father of the family and kind-hearted fool.*

Karpov, Korchnoi, and Kasparov: the Battle of the K's

After Bobby Fischer had relinquished the world chess championship title in 1975 by refusing to play against the Russian grandmaster Anatoly Karpov, the Russian was declared the new world champion. He retained the title for ten years, defending the title four times.

His opponent for the first two matches was a fellow Russian grandmaster, Victor Korchnoi. Karpov retained the title on both occasions. At this time chess computers were beginning to make an impact on the tournament scene. They were, for the first time,

The mischievous Bart Simpson appears as the pawn—multiplied sixteen times on the board, he could only cause havoc. The juxtaposition of this family and chess must be an intentional joke.

being entered into an occasional weekend event, mainly to provide their manufacturers with information as to their true chess strength. Computers did win a few games, but their usual position would be close to the bottom of the tournament table.

In 1984, Karpov began the defense of his title against a new young challenger, Garry Kasparov. The match winner would be the first player to win six games. Kasparov had qualified for the match by impressively winning matches against strong grandmaster opposition. With his confidence raised, he expected to continue this successful run against the champion. However, after the first nine games the score stood at Karpov 4, Kasparov 0, with five games drawn. Kasparov, embarrassed by his score, changed tactics: he started playing cautiously, obtaining one draw after another, and, after a further 17 games, Karpov won again. He now needed only one more win for the match.

Kasparov continued his drawing tactic and eventually was rewarded when he won the 32nd game. There were another 14 draws before a further result: Kasparov won his second game, and this was followed immediately by another win. The score now stood at Karpov 5, Kasparov 3. At this score the match was stopped by Florencio Campomanes, president of FIDE, the Fédération Internationale des Échecs (the World Chess Federation). The match had lasted five months and it was obvious that both players were exhausted. Also, the length of the contest had become an international embarrassment to the chess authorities.

A new match was arranged for the following year and restricted to a maximum of 24 games. The first player to score $12^1/_2$ points would be the winner. Kasparov was better prepared for his opponent and won a close match to become, at the age of 22, the youngest person to be world chess champion.

BELOW *Karpov and Kasparov play one of the many games they had to play against each other between 1984 and 1990. They dominated the chess world, having to face each other in five world championship matches. During this period they played each other 144 times. The total result was that Kasparov won 21, drew 104, lost 19. Despite the narrow result of only a two-game difference, Kasparov retained the world champion title throughout.*

Digital dominance: Garry and the gigabytes

However there was to be an unexpected challenge from an artificial source. Computer technology was improving annually and rapidly reaching a standard of play that was becoming formidable, even threatening the expertise of chess grandmasters.

The first chess computers available to the public were tabletop designs, exactly like a normal chess set and board, but

with an inbuilt computer chip that indicated which moves to play. These had reached a fairly good standard of competence when Microsoft swept across the world with its advanced computer systems. Chess programs became available on disk—and appeared to be able to do anything. Kasparov became an enthusiastic supporter, developing his own programs to provide essential records and information to assist his preparations for chess matches and tournaments.

Now many companies have produced chess programs on disk that provide a range of chess sets with which one can choose to play, and all offer a standard set, although the colors of such sets are no longer limited to black versus white. The chessmen are no longer seen as being boring, just moving from square to square: they jump, fly, slide, or even, which is popular with the younger generation, on capture blow up the square and the opposing warrior. The themes of the computer chess sets are legion, drawn from ancient empires, based on mythological legends, or on intergalactic warfare between alien empires. Computer chess sets are designed to be visually entertaining and exciting; there are no regulatory restrictions to dampen the aesthetic power of the imaginations of their programers.

In 1997 IBM Computers challenged the world chess champion Garry Kasparov to a second match against a machine called Deep Blue. The previous year Deep Blue had been beaten and human dignity was preserved: our champion had made a monkey of the monster machine. But now Kasparov, as the chosen champion to uphold the honor of the human race, had to face an even more colossal-megabyte Deep Blue, one that had, since its previous defeat, been reprogrammed with the help of some treacherous human grandmasters so that it was capable of calculating possible moves further ahead.

The first game our champion won; the second was worrying for the human race, because our champion lost. Games three, four, and five were draws. Kasparov was finding the battle much more difficult this time, and appeared not to be playing to his highest standard. After game three our champion was not amused to read in the *New York Times* a quote from an IBM executive stating, "I think we should look at this match as a chess match between the world's greatest chess player and Garry Kasparov." This may have been a contributing factor in unsettling Kasparov's concentration when everything depended on this sixth and last game.

It was a case of "winner take all"—and loss meant disaster, not only for Kasparov but also for the human race! The unimaginable happened: our champion lost, and for the first time since the creation of the universe a human lost an intellectual argument with another "species" of intelligence. And, embarrassingly, it was to a mindless machine that does not think for itself and has no knowledge or understanding of its achievement. Neither is there a possibility of another chance for our champion to recover the dignity of his race: Deep Blue has retired from chess competition and will not play again. The dastardly thing knows it would have little chance of beating Kasparov a second time. Or would it?

ABOVE Two old stars of the silver screen battle against each other over the chess board in the 1951 film The Great Man Hunt. *Douglas Fairbanks, Jr., appears to have the better game against Jack Hawkins, who seems baffled by the Chinese chessmen they are playing with.*

BELOW A modern artist displays in an old-fashioned format the way that the chess battles of the future will be presented to a mass audience.

Check and Mate and the game is finished,
—*Russian proverb*

INDEX

ACKNOWLEDGMENTS

I have drawn heavily on one thousand years of chess literature in the process of compiling this cameo kaleidoscope of the game's fascinating past. My appreciation goes to all those writers who have trodden this route before, sharing with future generations their time, knowledge, and dedication for chess.
My thanks also to members of Chess Collectors International who have been so active in recent years in researching the cultural and social history of the game and being so generous in sharing their discoveries with their fellow members. In particular, my grateful thanks to my wife, Vel, for bullying me throughout to keep to a strict timetable, editing each day's writing, and generally acting as my personal secretary.